THE LAST TRAIN FROM ESTONIA

A Memoir

Jaak Jurison

KURNI PRESS

Library of Congress Control Number 2016901115

Kurni Press, Newport Beach, California

ISBN 13 978-0692619902

ISBN 10 0692619909

Cover design by Denise Wada

This book is dedicated to

My father, Karl Jürison, whose optimism and passion for honor and integrity guided me throughout the formative years of my life.

My uncle, Haakon Raudsepp, whose able leadership was crucial in our escape from Soviet occupation in September of 1944.

The soldiers of the Estonian Legion, whose courageous efforts kept the Red Army at bay long enough to allow thousands of Estonians to escape.

Those who do not remember the past are condemned to repeat it.

—*George Santayana*

Contents

Prologue

I T IS A perfect September day in Finland. The blue sky over Helsinki Harbor is scattered with occasional white clouds, and the light breeze from the sea is cool and refreshing. I can sense a hint of autumn in the air. My wife and I are standing on the pier waiting to board *Tallink*, the hydrofoil vessel that will take us fifty miles across the Gulf of Finland to Tallinn, the capital of Estonia. A few seagulls glide in the sky, wailing as if they are sad to see us leave.

I feel an overwhelming sense of excitement, the kind I have not experienced since our wedding day. We are embarking upon a long-awaited, emotional journey. After being away for fifty years, we are returning to our homeland, Estonia.

"Are you as excited about this trip as I am?" I ask Siret.

"I don't know. I have mixed emotions," she replies. "I was only seven when I left and have just a few faint memories of my childhood home. But you were older. You must have more memories."

I have, indeed. I was thirteen when I left—or more accurately, fled—my home. I remember well how my carefree childhood abruptly ended with Soviet Russia's takeover of Estonia in 1940. I have vivid recollections of the events that took place in the years that followed. It is impossible to forget what happened in those terrible times under both the Soviet and Nazi occupations.

Siret and I board the vessel and find two seats with views of Helsinki's scenic harbor and the tiny surrounding islands. Most of the passengers around us seem to be Finns intent on a shopping spree to Estonia, where many goods and alcoholic beverages—vodka and beer—are known to be much cheaper than in Finland. There are hardly any Estonians on board, judging by the language of overheard conversations.

As we leave the archipelago, I lean back to collect my thoughts. This is a day I have often dreamed of—to return to an Estonia that is free from foreign occupation and tyranny. It was only four years ago, in 1991, when the country became independent again amid the collapse of the communist Soviet Union. What will I find there now? What is left of the places where I spent my childhood and went to school? What will my two cousins be like after having survived two rounds of deportations to Siberia? Will I even recognize them?

I get up and step to the forward deck, anxiously hoping to catch the first glimpse of the Estonian coastline. It is still hidden behind the horizon that separates a blue sky from the gray waters of the gulf. Finally, the dark contours of the coastline emerge from the haze.

Thrilled beyond belief, I shout to a crew member standing next to me, "This is my homeland! I haven't seen it for many years."

He looks at me and nonchalantly asks, "So when did you leave?"

"Fifty years ago, almost exactly to this date," I reply.

"That must have been about the time when the Russians came back. I wasn't born then, but my father told me all about it."

"Yes. I managed to get on the last train before the Soviet tanks rolled into Tallinn."

Showing more interest, he asks, "Where did you go then? I understand that most people escaped either to Sweden or Germany."

"We fled from one island to another, looking for ways to go to Sweden. But we were too late. Anyone with a boat big enough to cross the Baltic Sea had already left. So we ended up in Germany ten days later."

"What did you do there?"

"We went to the central part of Germany, to avoid getting caught in battles at the eastern and western fronts. After surviving horrendous Allied bombings in the city, we moved to a small village, where I saw the arrival of the first American troops."

"It must have been a happy moment."

"Indeed it was. But the joy was short-lived because the Americans turned that part of Germany over to the Russians, and we had to flee once again. We escaped to an area under British military control and ended up in a displaced-persons' camp in Oldenburg. We lived in abandoned military barracks. We had our own Estonian schools, church services, and many cultural activities. I finished Gymnasium there, and then I was lucky to emigrate to America and start a new life—with only two dollars in my pocket."

"And then you quickly became rich like all Americans," the crewman says. "We see them all the time on television shows like *Santa Barbara* and *Dallas*."

"Oh, no, no. Not everyone is rich in America. We had to work very hard just to make a living. I worked my way through college and also served in the American Army at the end of the Korean War."

"So what are you doing now?"

"Now I am a professor at Fordham University in New York City. I just finished lecturing at the Turku School of Economics two days ago."

"You must have had a very interesting life. You should write a book about it."

"Well, you aren't the only one to suggest that," I reply, thinking that someday I might actually do that.

"Look, there's the Estonian coast," he shouts and points at the shoreline ahead

The details of the shoreline become clearer now, and I can see the outline of Tallinn, the city where I was born. I rush to the cabin to get Siret and my camera. We stand at the bow with our eyes fixed on the view ahead. I start snapping photos, but even with a zoom lens, the buildings still look too distant. I wait until I can discern major landmarks—the familiar church steeples and medieval towers I recall from pre-war postcards. The silhouettes of the towering Saint Olaf and the smaller Saint Nicholas churches are unmistakable.

We are entering the harbor, and my heart beats faster the closer we get to the pier. I can't wait to disembark. Finally, we walk down the gangplank and enter a gray, nondescript building, where we stand in line to clear customs. We receive the usual routine from the agent. "What is the purpose of your trip? How long do you plan to stay?" Noting that we were both born in Estonia, he returns our passports with a smile and says, *"Tere tulemast koju."* How beautiful to hear these words: "Welcome home." Only a few years earlier I couldn't even imagine returning to the land of my birth—a land that is now finally free from foreign occupation. And now here we are.

We pass through the exit door to face a small, welcoming crowd. It takes me a few moments before I recognize my cousin Eda, her face beaming behind a colorful bouquet of flowers. Our families were torn apart fifty-three years ago, when we she was only ten. She was among the hapless Estonians who were rounded up in the middle of the night by Soviet agents and deported to the desolate steppes of Siberia. For many years, I had lost all hope of seeing her again. It is hard to believe that she is standing in front of me now—no longer the child that I remembered, but a mature woman. The years spent in Siberia have not marred her sweet smile nor extinguished the sparkle in her eyes.

I give her a long, hearty bear hug. I introduce Siret, and they embrace as if they have known each other for a long time. As I wipe tears from my cheeks, I notice that Siret's eyes are tearful as well. Suddenly, I realize that we are really back in our homeland and that my dream finally has been fulfilled.

We head toward the parking lot, where Eda's nephew is waiting in his car. With our eyes still misty, we begin the drive to Eda's home. As we pass through several neighborhoods, I try to glimpse familiar landmarks. Unable to find any, I begin to feel like a stranger in a foreign land. With the exception of the church steeples in the city's skyline, everything seems different from my childhood days.

We leave the main thoroughfare and enter a quiet residential area. "We are already in Nõmme, our hometown," Eda announces. As we turn into a small street with overgrown bushes amidst tall pine trees, she looks at me and asks, "Do you remember this street?"

"No, not really," I reply. "Where are we?"

"You don't remember?" Eda chuckles. "This is the street where you lived."

"Really?" I ask in disbelief. "We never had such tall trees and big bushes on our street."

"Look to the left now," says Eda. She points to a two-story house that is partially hidden behind bushes. "This is the house where you lived."

We stop for a closer look. I gaze at the rusting roof and the front door that looms next to a row of three windows. Suddenly, it appears that someone has pushed the fast-backward button on my brain and all the intervening years have faded away. This is, indeed, the house where I grew up. Behind the window beside the front door was my father's study with his dark oak desk and massive leather chairs. Behind the middle window was the guest room where my grandparents and occasional visitors would stay. The corner room on the left is my room, where I was awakened by morning sunlight, and the adjacent terrace, where I played games with friends. Here is the place of my earliest memories. Here I enjoyed my happy childhood, cut short by the Second World War, which destroyed countless millions of lives.

This book is based on my memory of what took place during those tumultuous times. It is a story about an Estonian boy who lived under both Soviet and Nazi occupations, escaped the onslaught of Soviet tanks, and miraculously survived devastating bomb attacks. It shows how it is possible to endure difficult challenges, and how resilience, ingenuity, love, and luck can change our lives in many unexpected ways. It is my story.

However, it is more than a personal account. The historical context I have provided reflects much of what happened to citizens of the three small Baltic countries—Estonia, Latvia, and Lithuania—caught in the fighting between the armies of two ruthless dictators, Hitler and Stalin. First seized by Soviet Russia, then occupied by Germany, and later fallen again under Soviet control, people suffered greatly during those years. I was among the lucky ones able to escape the second Soviet occupation and tell the world what really happened. There are many others who have similar stories to tell, but only a few have been published. My story is unique because I witnessed firsthand the tragic events that unfolded from the day the war started through the difficult years that followed. I was old enough to understand what was happening and the agonizing decisions that people were forced to make.

I believe the history of the Baltic States is more relevant today than ever. Though the world is vastly different now, menacing new clouds are rising on the horizon. They are reminiscent of the time when the Second World War began. I hope that my personal story will in some ways serve as a warning about future threats to people of the free and democratic world.

1

Beginnings

B Y THE TIME I was born, the guns of war had been silent for a decade. Although the First World War ended officially on November 11, 1918, the hostilities did not stop in Estonia, a small country of about a million people sandwiched between Russia and the Baltic Sea. After declaring independence on February 24, 1918, Estonians still had to fight the German forces in the South and the Soviet Army in the East for another two years, until Russia signed the Tartu Peace Treaty on February 2, 1920. Under this treaty, Soviet Russia agreed to recognize the independence and territorial rights of the Republic of Estonia in perpetuity. The War of Independence, or literally, the Freedom War (*Vabadussõda*), brought sovereignty and the freedom to determine their own destiny to a people who had been since the thirteenth century dominated by various conquerors—the German and Danish crusaders early on, followed by Swedish kings and Russian czars. Estonia finally established itself as an independent nation, and became a full member of the League of Nations, in 1921. Estonians, like most people around the world, hoped the League would maintain peace and stability and prevent future wars.

Once the destruction and damage from the War of Independence had been repaired, the country embarked on a swift economic recovery. It was boosted by countrywide land reform, which created a large number of privately owned farms. People were enthusiastic and proud of their newly acquired national identity, brimming with hope and optimism. Estonian creativity exploded, and cultural life—literature, music, art, and theater—flourished in ways that would have been un-thinkable in the past. The future looked bright, and opportunities seemed unlimited.

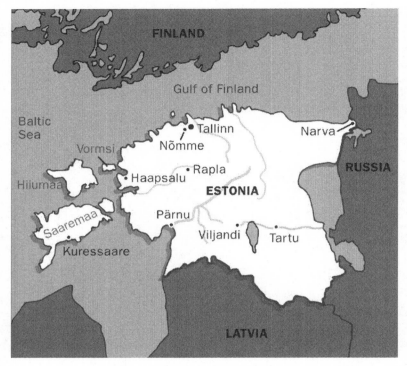

1928 was a particularly good year. A Soviet-sponsored communist coup attempted four years earlier had been successfully averted, and confidence in the government was high. Just as the stock market in the United States was reaching new heights, the Estonian people also enjoyed a rise in prosperity and security. Estonian athletes competed in the Olympic Games in Amsterdam and brought home five medals, including two gold. This was a great achievement for a small country, and it gave a further boost to the sense of national pride and identity. This was also the year my parents got married.

My father was a young pharmacist at the beginning of a promising career. His family was from a region called Mulgimaa whose inhabi-tants were considered to be frugal, shrewd, and often wealthy. They were among the early leaders in an awakening national movement that supported teaching in the Estonian language in high schools and the use of Estonian in other cultural endeavors. Most of them were thrifty farm workers who became early buyers of farmland from the Baltic German landowners after serfdom was abolished in the beginning of the nineteenth century. And then luck smiled on them. The Civil War that interrupted cotton production in America caused the demand for linen to soar. The farmers started growing flax and became wealthy by selling it at inflated prices on the open market in Riga (now the capital of Latvia).

My grandparents, Jüri and Kadri Jürison, were not as affluent as the entrepreneurial farmers. Still, they were relatively well off, living in the town of Viljandi, where they owned a bed-and-breakfast inn. It catered to traveling farmers and business people and included a restaurant, a bar, and a courtyard for keeping horses and carriages. Grandfather managed the inn, tended the bar, and socialized with customers; Grandmother was in charge of the kitchen. Regrettably, I never had a chance to meet her because she died before I was born.

Their only son was my father, Karl Jürison. He was born at the turn of the century, on October 23, 1900. His sister Alide, Aunt Iti, was born eight years later. After finishing high school, my father served as a medic in the War of Independence. When the war was over, his parents used their savings to send him to the University of Tartu to study pharmacy at the medical school.

My mother, Alma, was born and raised in Tartu, the second largest Estonian city. It was well known for its university, which was founded by Swedish King Gustav II Adolf in 1632. She was the second of four children of Karl and Ida (née Undritz) Ratassepp. They owned and operated Hotel Tartu, a three-story hotel within easy reach of the Town Hall, across the Stone Bridge. My maternal grandfather passed away at an early age, leaving the hotel's management responsibilities to his wife, Ida. She was an extraordinarily talented and courageous woman whom I got to know and deeply admire in my later years. Her ancestors came from Sweden during the sixteenth century and included several accomplished teachers and clergymen.

My mother had three siblings: an older sister, Elsbeth (Aunt Elli); a younger sister, Senta; and a brother, Karl (Uncle Karli), the youngest.

My grandparents, Jüri and Kadri Jürison, with their
son Karl (my father) and daughter Alide (Aunt Iti)

My parents met while my mother was attending cooking school after graduating from the Tartu Girls' Gymnasium. She was not allowed to follow her dream of going to university because her father thought that only sons should be given such opportunities. Girls were expected to get married and become good housewives—so off to cooking school she went. The school had a restaurant where the apprentice cooks served whatever fare they'd prepared in the kitchen on that particular day. It was popular with local university students, including my father, who was a regular customer. He soon noticed a slender girl with dark hair and brown eyes and, it seems, my mother found his blond hair and blue eyes just as attractive.

Their courtship lasted three years and included ice-skating dates in winter and tennis dates in summer. Ice-skating was a proper way for a young man to court a girl in those days. According to my mother, they took special pleasure in many romantic twilight boat rides on the Emajõgi, a river that has been glorified in many popular songs. They also enjoyed dances and other social events at the house of my father's fraternity, Fraternitas Liviensis. The town of Tartu had a vibrant social life organized mainly around student fraternities and sororities, whose ubiquitous members brightened the street scene by wearing caps with their individual fraternity or sorority colors.

Shortly after my father completed his master's thesis, they were married on February 18, 1928, in Saint Paul's church in Tartu. Judging from the thick stack of congratulatory telegrams I discovered in my cousin's home on a recent visit, I believe that the party celebrating their wedding must have been relatively small, with only family members and close friends in attendance.

The newlyweds moved to Tallinn, where my father managed a small pharmacy. Two years later, he became partner in a large private pharmacy near the Town Hall. They moved into a larger apartment on Poska Street in Kadriorg, a pleasant residential neighborhood within steps of historic Kadriorg Park. Shortly thereafter, I was born, on May 6, 1931.

According to my mother, choosing a name did not come easily. My father wanted me to have a true Estonian name, like Peep, Priit, or Lembit. At the height of the nationwide patriotism of that time, giving newborn babies Estonian names was *de rigueur*. Even many adults with foreign last names "Estonianized" them by adopting Estonian-sounding names. But my mother insisted that they consider how the name would sound in foreign countries, particularly in English-speaking ones. She apparently had a premonition that fate would take me to a faraway foreign land. How right she was. So they compromised on Jaak, an Estonian name derived from Jakob that could easily morph into Jack in London or New York. As a toddler, I was called Jässu. It still puzzles me how I got that name, which I never learned to like. I tolerated it until the first day of school, when I declared that from that day on I was Jaak, and Heaven have mercy on anyone who dared call me Jässu.

With my parents when I was still called Jässu

2

Childhood Memories

MY EARLIEST CHILDHOOD memory is of the day when my family moved from our home in Kadriorg. Moving to a new home can be unsettling for a three-year-old, and that's probably why I still remember it. I recall many big boxes, about my height or even taller, filling the hallway and getting in my way. And to make things worse, all of my favorite toys had disappeared into those boxes.

I remember the automobile ride to our new home, a two-family house on Kurni Street in Nõmme, a suburb about four miles south of the city center. The new home had an enormous yard where I could frolic among pine trees and play in my own sandbox. What more could a boy want at that age? According to my mother, I had no difficulty adjusting to this new environment, which became my home for the next seven years.

We lived on the first floor. The second floor was occupied by the owners of the building, the Benksons—an elderly German couple who spoke Estonian with a distinct German accent. Most of the time, they kept to themselves and we had little contact with them.

The entry to our apartment led to a long hallway that was the central hub of our home. On the left wall was a telephone with a loud, distinctive ring. It was mounted so high that I couldn't reach it without standing on a chair. At the end of the hallway, separated by French doors, was a large living room with a dining table where we ate our midday dinner and evening supper. On one side of the living room was my parents' bedroom, and on the opposite side was my room. The yellow wallpaper gave my room a cheerful feeling, especially in the early morning, when it almost glowed in bright sunlight. In one corner of the living room, a glass door opened up to the terrace and the garden.

My childhood home in Nõmme

There were two additional rooms along the hallway. One was used as a guest room where my grandparents and other relatives stayed during their visits. The other room was my father's study, replete with his desk, bookshelves, and furniture. The bookshelves were filled with professional journals and the latest books by Estonian authors, along with such foreign literary works as *Buddenbrooks*, *Gone with the Wind*, and *The Good Earth*. The furniture consisted of a massive leather sofa and two leather chairs in the typical British style, as seen years later in the last few episodes of the *Upstairs, Downstairs* TV series. Like many Estonian families at the time, we were greatly influenced by British culture, fashions, and decor. The study was used also for entertaining and for serving after-dinner drinks when we had company. To my disappointment, I was usually excluded from such occasions because they lasted well beyond my bedtime.

When my father was not at his desk, I was allowed to play the Blaupunkt radio console that stood majestically in one corner. The choice of Estonian-language programs was limited to what was broadcast on the national radio station—mostly classical music, news, and a few radio plays. But by twiddling the tuning knob, I could listen to any foreign station listed on the dial and was in this way able to learn the names of almost every European capital from Riga to Rome. Another technical marvel I loved to operate was the gramophone. It required extreme care to position the needle, and the gramophone had to be rewound after each record. I still remember the record labels showing a picture of a cute dog listening intensely to "His Master's Voice" from the horn of a gramophone.

Across the hallway from my father's study was the kitchen, and across from the guest room was the bathroom. The wood-burning water heater in the kitchen served both of these rooms. The kitchen stove and all furnaces were heated by burning wood or briquettes made from oil shale. Briquettes were popular in Estonia because of the abundant oil shale reserves in the northeastern part of the country. Behind the kitchen was the maid's room. We had a live-in maid who cooked, cleaned, and tried to keep me out of mischief, the latter being perhaps the most demanding part of her duties.

Overall, our home was comfortable and functional, with adequate space for a young boy to play and run around. In good weather, I loved to play outside in the yard. The homes in Nõmme were built in a pine forest and most of the trees were preserved when the area was developed. Therefore, we had lots of pine trees and squirrels in our yard. It was a pure joy to watch those friendly creatures scamper and leap gracefully from one tree branch to another. One day I left the front door open, and to my delight—and my parents' horror—a young squirrel sneaked into the house. I can't recall any other day when we had such chaos in our home. Everyone was chasing the frightened creature, who kept desperately looking for cover under beds and sofas until it eventually found its way to freedom.

The front of the house was landscaped with small bushes amid a row of pine trees. A few steps down a small slope to the backyard there were more pine trees, a few young apple trees, and some open space. Part of that space was set aside for a vegetable garden, where we grew strawberries, raspberries, and three types of currants—red, white, and black. I can still remember the pungent smell and flavor of the juicy black currants. We also grew vegetables, ranging from string beans to carrots, peas, and even small red potatoes.

One corner of the garden belonged to me. This was the place where I could grow my own flowers and berries. I took my gardening responsibilities very seriously. Every morning I checked the plants, watered and weeded as necessary. My gardening efforts paid off well—whatever seeds I sowed, the plants flourished. The joy of harvesting my first strawberries was unforgettable.

Encouraged by my success, I decided to try my luck with growing candy. I thought it was a brilliant idea. No longer would I need to ask my parents for candy because I would have my own supply. Despite my parents' discouragement, I insisted that my idea would work. So I took a bag of strawberry candy, which had a seed-like semblance, and dropped each candy neatly into well-prepared soil, watered diligently, and waited for the first sprouts to appear. I waited and waited, watered and fertilized, and waited some more. Still not a single sprout. Finally, I had to admit that my parents were right and my experiment had failed. It was a hard pill for a know-it-all kid to swallow.

Most of my preschool days were spent with my mother and our maid, Marie. She was a cranky, middle-aged woman who often bossed me around when we were alone. Obviously, we didn't get along well. I was overjoyed when my mother replaced her with a pretty, young girl named Vera. She and I got along fabulously; she taught me the latest popular songs and even shared a few secrets about her romantic adventures.

I couldn't find any playmates on our street because none of our neighbors had children close to my age. My only playmate in those days was my cousin Eda, who was one year older. She and her mother, Aunt Elli, lived nearby, and we played whenever our mothers decided to get together. Her older brother, Ilmar, was already going to school and had better things to do than playing with us "babies."

Therefore, it is not surprising that that I sought my father's company whenever he was around. He came home regularly for the midday dinner and an occasional nap before returning to work. I waited eagerly for his arrival, like a puppy waiting for his master. I remember him being immaculately dressed, thanks to my mother's good taste in clothing. He wore dark suits in winter, light gray suits in summer, spats, and shirts with removable collars, as was customary in those days. Being a pharmacist, he brought home the scents of the pharmacy—a blend of elixirs and herbal medications. Even now, every time I visit a traditional European pharmacy, that same intoxicating aroma brings back fond memories. When my father asked whether I had been a good boy while he was at work, I believe that on many occasions I stretched the truth in order to see his approving smile.

According to my recollection, I always ate dinner with my parents. I was expected to behave and demonstrate good table manners. Thanks to my mother's cooking-school experience, we always had a well-balanced diet, with plenty of vegetables and a meatless day once a week. However, I do remember a time when my father was put on a special diet for his ulcers. All of us ate a bland, creamy rice soup until his ulcers healed. I couldn't have been happier that he recovered quickly.

Because my father spent long hours at the pharmacy, I often didn't see him in the evenings. This made Sundays, when he was home, special occasions. My father would take time to play with me, tell fascinating stories, and fix my broken toys. In summer we played ball in the backyard, while in winter we went sledding on the snowy slopes in the neighborhood. Occasionally, he would ask me to get him cigarettes from a nearby newsstand. Proud to be trusted with such a responsibility, I was more than happy to do it. His favorite brand was Eva; it came in a green package with a picture of a woman in the left-hand corner.

When the weather was good, my parents would take me for leisurely Sunday walks in the neighborhood. On the way home, we would stop by a little market across the train station and buy tea biscuits, which we munched in my parents' bedroom until there was nothing left but crumbs scattered all over the bed. Those were precious moments.

While my father was busy at work, my mother had plenty of time to spend with me. As the only child, I got much attention from her—much more than I thought I needed. Sometimes I wished I had a couple of siblings so that my mother would spend more time with them and worry less about me. She was a loving and caring mother with ambitious plans for my future. She expected me to go to the University of Tartu and study pharmacy like my father, so that I could take over managing his pharmacy in time. (According to Estonian law, only pharmacists could own pharmacies.)

She had high hopes that I would achieve success and happiness in a peaceful world. She abhorred wars. She told me that innocent people get killed in wars, and that's why she hoped we would never have to experience one. She had grown up during the First World War, and the horrors she saw had left an indelible mark on her. When her hometown Tartu was briefly overrun by the Soviet Army during the War of Independence, she had witnessed unbelievable brutalities.

My father, on the other hand, did not share her anti-war sentiment. He felt that some wars, notably the war for Estonian independence, were justified, despite their casualties. He was proud of his service and was a member of the Defense League—a voluntary organization formed after the failed communist coup—to quell future threats to the country's independence.

Both of my parents strongly believed in the importance of education and in knowledge of foreign languages. Living in a small European country, an educated person was expected to be literate in several foreign languages. Anyone who wanted to travel, study, or do business abroad had to be passably fluent in at least one major European language. My mother was truly multilingual; she was able to read, write, and converse in Russian, German, English, and to some degree, in French. My father's mastery of foreign languages was less remarkable, limited only to Russian and German.

When it came time to enter kindergarten, both my cousin Eda and I went to a bilingual one taught by a German lady, Tante (Aunt) Heddi. We played games and sang songs in both Estonian and German. The sounds of "O Tannenbaum, O Tannenbaum" still ring clearly in my ears during the Christmas holidays. Unfortunately, I missed many classes because I caught my share of all the childhood diseases prevalent at that time: measles, chickenpox, whooping cough, and mumps. Miraculously, I escaped scarlet fever. I remember spending much time in my room alone in bed—no visitors were allowed, to avoid the spread of germs. Those were the most boring days of my childhood. There was not much to do other than read, look at the snow banks through my window, and dream of summer days, when my father would take time off from work and we would go on vacation to some faraway place.

The farthest we went in my early childhood, however, was Uncle Karli's farm, Sulbi, about thirty miles southeast of Tartu. To get there, we had to take a train from Tallinn to Tartu, where Uncle Karli would meet us with a horse-drawn carriage. Then it would take a good part of the day, including a river crossing by a small ferry, to reach his farm.

Uncle Karli and his wife Olga (Aunt Olli) had a spacious farmhouse where we enjoyed the pleasures of life on their farm; no running water, but plenty of fresh fruits, and a good sauna a few steps away from the house. A short downhill path led to a winding river. Its water flow was interrupted by a dam that powered a mill—a combination of sawmill and flour mill—and provided electricity for the farmhouse. A wide meadow on the upstream side of the riverbank was an ideal place to spend leisurely summer days. My mother would read or swim in the calm waters, while my father preferred fishing or taking us for rides in a small rowboat.

Vacationing in Sulbi. From left are Aunt Elli, Cousin Eda, her
father Uncle Artur, my mother and I, Cousin Ilmar,
Grandmother Ida, and my father

Back home, I relished the days when my mother and I ventured into
the city to visit my father's pharmacy, an outing that was always
thrilling and fun. We would take a bus to the city, get off near the
Estonia Theater, and walk a few blocks to my father's pharmacy. It
was around the corner from the Town Hall Square, on Suur Karja 4,
directly across from an imposing building, the Scheel Bank, the largest private bank in Estonia. There was a wide archway with two
entrances: the one on the left was for a café with a mouth-watering
window display of cakes and cookies, the right one led to the
pharmacy.

The moment we stepped into the pharmacy, we were greeted by
that distinctive scent—the same unmistakable one I smelled on my
father's clothes when he came home for dinner. A couple of pharmacists in white laboratory coats would always greet us from behind the
enormous service counter that extended along the entire room. On the
shelf behind the counter were test tubes, scales and measuring devices
for formulating prescriptions, and a typewriter for printing labels.
Along the back wall stood shelves and glass-enclosed cabinets full of
bottles and jars. There was always someone on hand to give me a

tour, explain what the pharmacists did, and show how they filled prescriptions. I believe the reason for those tours was to stoke my interest in pharmacy at an early age and encourage me to follow in my father's footsteps.

The visits were never complete without stopping by the café across the gangway. My mother and I would enjoy some delectable pastries with tea, and we always bought more for taking home. I thought they made the best meringues and chocolate cookies in the world. Still, to this day, I am not sure which I enjoyed more—visiting the pharmacy or the café.

I loved those visits so much that one day I decided, as a five- or six-year-old, to go all by myself. I took my tiny suitcase, filled it with a few half-empty bottles from the medicine cabinet, and announced to my mother, who was busy in the kitchen: "I am going to the pharmacy with some empty bottles."

"Oh, that's nice, she mumbled. Pleased to have her permission, I grabbed my suitcase and left for the bus station.

When the bus arrived, I stood back and let other passengers board first. When my turn came, the bus driver looked at me and asked, "Where do you think you are going?"

"To visit my father in Tallinn," I replied.

"And where is your mother?"

"At home."

"Then go home and come back with her," said the driver and closed the door in my face.

Dismayed and frustrated, I started to shuffle back home. Suddenly, I saw my mother running toward me, waving her arms and screaming, "Where have you been?"

"I was going to see my father in the pharmacy."

"You never told me that. How could you leave without my permission?" she yelled, her face red from anger.

"But I did," I tried to explain. By that time, my father was approaching us from the opposite end of the street. He had rushed home by taxi after my mother had called to report me missing. He appeared just as upset as my mother, and demanded an explanation for my presumed misbehavior.

"I told mother that I was going to see you and bring some bottles with me," I explained.

Despite all my efforts, I was unable to convince him that I had her permission. She insisted that she had never given it to me, thinking that I was just playing at going to the pharmacy. My father thought that I had lied, and therefore, I deserved to be punished. As he whipped my buttocks with the traditional punishing switch, I cried and protested vehemently. I felt deeply hurt and insulted by this unfair treatment. I had followed the rules and still been punished.

That was one of the rare moments when I was punished by my father. The task of correcting my minor misbehaviors was usually left to my mother, who did not shirk from that responsibility. But on that day, I believe, my father saw an opportunity to teach me a lesson in what he considered an important part in my upbringing—instilling integrity and honesty in me. He had no tolerance for lying or dishonest behavior and often talked about the importance of honesty and trustworthiness, quoting an old Estonian proverb: "*Meest sõnast, härga sarvist*" (A man is judged by his word, a bull by his horns). His insistence on keeping one's word influenced me so much that, to this day, I am reluctant to make promises unless I am convinced that I can keep them.

I recall another incident that almost got me into trouble with my father, but in an entirely different way. He had imported seedlings of special herbs by mail order. I don't recall whether they came from Sweden or Germany, but they were rare and very expensive. My father was thrilled when they arrived. He tilled and prepared the soil in a corner of our garden for planting them over the coming weekend. "They're very special. They have to be handled with extreme care," he said.

The following day, after my father had left for work, I decided to be a good boy and do him a favor. I took the seedlings and planted them, one by one, in the selected spot in the garden. When my mother saw my handiwork, she was horrified. "Father saved this job for himself," she said. "You better hope that that the seedlings won't die, otherwise both of us will be in trouble."

When my father came home and heard what I had done, he looked displeased. "Please don't worry," I said. "I planted them very carefully." After he had examined the row of freshly planted seedlings, he calmed down and said, "What is done is done. We can't do anything more than take good care of them. I'm sure they will grow." I watered them as faithfully as I had watered my candy and prayed they would survive. To everyone's surprise and delight, all of the plants not only survived, but flourished.

I was grateful for my father's calm handling of the situation. He had a marvelous ability to see the bright side in every situation. His positive outlook on life was a refreshing contrast to my mother's cautious personality. My father took pride in being an optimist and encouraged me to adopt his sanguine attitude. "Be an optimist. Don't be a pessimist," he advised. When I asked him what the word "pessimist" meant, he told me the following story:

It was a tale of two frogs. One was an optimist, the other a pessimist. They happened to fall into a jar full of fresh cream. The pessimist sighed and said, "This is the end. We'll never get out of here," and drowned. The optimist, on the other hand, decided not to give up. He kept struggling, kicking his legs until the cream eventually churned into butter and he was able to jump out of the jar.

"Whenever you are sad and unhappy," my father said, "think about the frogs." The point he made has been with me ever since.

3

Starting School

I STARTED SCHOOL at the age of seven, one year earlier than most of my classmates. My parents had planned to send me to the English College, a private school in Tallinn with emphasis on teaching English, but considered me too young to travel alone to the city. So I went to the public elementary school within walking distance from home, with plans to transfer to the English College two years later.

I fell in love with school on day one, quickly made new friends, and was delighted to have a boy named Heiki as my benchmate. He lived near my home, and we became good friends. All the boys had to wear caps with the school's colors; ours were dark green with a yellow brim. We were expected to wear them with pride and dignity, and only on cold winter days could we exchange them for fur hats with ear flaps. If a student misbehaved in public, bystanders would immediately know which school he attended and could report the incident to the school's administration. I recall one occasion when a couple of boys from our school had been reported for fighting on the street. All students were called to the auditorium and were not allowed to leave until the culprits were identified and disciplined.

Physical education played a major role in our school curriculum. We did gymnastics in winter and played *laptuu*, a game similar to softball, in spring and fall. In addition to our classroom lessons, we had daily homework assignments. At the beginning of the school

year, my mother checked every evening that I had completed my
homework and helped me if I needed assistance. She stopped doing
that as soon as she discovered it was no longer necessary, but we still
continued our daily discussions about various happenings at school.

One secret I kept from my mother for a long time was that I had a
crush on a beautiful, dark-haired girl who sat one row ahead of me;
the girl was named Pilvi. I thought she was really cute and kept
admiring her from a distance because I lacked the courage to
approach her directly. Despite her allure, I was able to concentrate on
schoolwork and received good grades in every subject except music.

I loved to sing, but somehow never managed to find the right key.
So I let others carry the tune while I moved my lips in the background. In addition to popular children's songs, we learned our
national anthem and the anthems of our friendly neighboring
countries—Latvia, Finland, and Sweden—in their native languages.

At the end of my first school year, my parents decided that I was old
enough for an adventurous vacation on the island of Vormsi, located
off the northwestern coast of Estonia. To get there, we had to take a
ferry from the mainland. Upon arrival, we were welcomed by local
women offering horse-drawn taxi service to the main village. Our
driver, clad in a colorful local costume, was an interesting woman. I
was struck by the way she managed to guide the horse (actually, the
horse knew the road very well), concentrate on knitting something
that looked like a sweater, and, at the same time, keep us entertained
with captivating stories about the island and its people. The quaint
island of thirty-five square miles was rich in Viking history and
culture. The islanders—descendants of the Swedish occupiers of the
seventeenth century—still spoke Swedish and maintained their
culture and traditions. There were no automobiles or gas stations on
the island.

The resort where we stayed consisted of clusters of cottages and a
covered open-air dining area with several communal dining tables. I
enjoyed the outdoor dining no less than the attention I received from
the many interesting grown-up guests. The two most memorable peo-

ple were a famous actress and a newspaper cartoonist, who loved to entertain the guests by drawing caricatures of them. I, too, posed for him, amazing my mother, who couldn't believe I was able to sit still that long.

Most of our days were spent hiking, since my father wanted us to explore the island by visiting every village on foot. Our paths went through endless patches of ever-present juniper trees; I still recall their strong fragrance whenever I enjoy a gin martini. Although some longer expeditions left me exhausted and sunburned, I felt proud to be able to meet the challenge and keep up with my parents.

The most exciting moment of this vacation was witnessing the arrival of the first automobile on the island. On a quiet afternoon, I heard the sound of an automobile horn. It's impossible, I thought, there are no autos here. But after the second toot I was on my way out to investigate. It really was an automobile—a black sedan parked at the main entrance, surrounded by a crowd of curious villagers. It belonged to the owner of our resort, a big cheerful man who enjoyed taking local village children for joyrides. When he heard of our interest in seeing the lighthouse at the other end of the island, he offered to drive us there. It was an offer we could not refuse. That trip gave us an opportunity to explore the remaining part of the island, making our vacation in Vormsi complete.

A few days after our return from vacation, another car—a shiny black Opel sedan—stopped unexpectedly in front of our house. "Look at our new automobile," shouted Eda as she stepped out of the car. She didn't have to say that because I was already marveling it from every possible angle. A car was still a novelty for me because we didn't have one. Eda's father, Uncle Artur, proudly demonstrated his magnificent driving machine by driving us through the neighborhood streets. As we returned home, I remember asking my father, "Why can't we have one?"

"We will have one, but not now. You have to wait a few years for that," he said, and explained that car ownership was a luxury we couldn't afford yet.

We actually didn't need a car because we had excellent bus and train service just a few short blocks away. Besides, Uncle Artur was always happy to take us on various day trips. On one of those trips we went to Pirita, a favorite seaside destination for Sunday outings, about four miles northeast of Tallinn. My mother packed sandwiches and lemonade in a wicker basket, and our two families—all seven of us— squeezed into Uncle Artur's automobile. We had a picnic in a meadow, played ball on the banks of Pirita River, and later walked on the beach. Before returning, we stopped at an ice-cream shop that served the most delicious ice cream. I thought it was the best in the world, served in cones and sprinkled with crushed nuts.

Longer trips included visits to Grandmother Ida in Tartu. We went there by train, taking along homemade sandwiches and drinks. Grandmother lived on the second floor of the three-story hotel that she owned and managed. I loved to sit on her balcony, which offered a clear view of the majestic eighteenth-century Stone Bridge. With her powerful telescope I could watch people, horse-drawn carriages, and automobiles as they crossed the bridge.

Grandmother's hotel in Tartu

Grandmother Ida

Grandmother had many interests. Her favorite hobby was designing and weaving rugs, which she gave as gifts to family members. She would take me to her studio and demonstrate how she worked with her enormous looms. Seeing that made me realize how much effort and love had gone into weaving the colorful rug that adorned our living room. She loved to tell stories about her life and explain how different things had been when she was young. One of her complaints was that modern popular songs weren't as good as those of her youth.

When the first snowflakes started to fall, Estonian children began to dream of Christmas. Some of those dreams stayed with us for a long time. I still remember the happiest Christmas of my childhood, when I was eight years old. It also happened to be the last Christmas when our small family was still together.

The anticipation and preparations started weeks before Christmas Day. At school, we discussed the meaning of Christmas and practiced

Christmas songs. At home, the season arrived with delivery of the Christmas tree. It occupied one whole corner in our living room, the top just short of the nine-foot ceiling. It was the biggest and most gorgeous tree that I recall ever having in our house. The task of decorating it consumed all my energies for several days.

My mother taught me how to make hanging ornaments from walnuts. First, we would carefully cut the shell into two halves, remove the nutmeat, and then glue the shells back together with a loop of string between them for hanging on the tree. The real fun came when we started painting the shells, usually in gold or silver. After the paint had dried, we hung them on the tree, along with fancier ornaments, tinsel, and small candles.

We used real wax candles. I don't believe electric Christmas lights were even available in those days. The candles had to be carefully positioned on the tree to prevent the branches from catching fire. The previous Christmas a house in our neighborhood had caught fire from a burning Christmas tree. I was frequently reminded of that as a warning to be careful with matches and fire.

The most important and holiest event of Christmas in Estonia is Christmas Eve. It is a time for families to be together, attend church services, sing Christmas carols, exchange gifts, and enjoy holiday food and drinks. My family was no exception. Grandfather Jüri and Aunt Iti joined my parents and me by the Christmas tree to sing "Silent Night" and several other Christmas carols. My favorite carol I learned at school that year was "Tasa, Tasa, Jõulukellad Kajavad" ("Softly, Softly, Christmas Bells are Ringing"). It had such a soft, melodic ring to it that even I could carry that tune.

Traditionally, Aunt Iti played the role of Santa Claus. She would arrive with a bag full of gifts, and only after being assured of my good behavior and listening to my Christmas recital, would she give them to me. Since I had uncovered her disguise a year earlier, the mystery of Santa Claus was gone, and Santa didn't visit us anymore. I felt that I had really arrived—I knew the truth about Santa and I no longer expected to receive children's toys.

Being an avid reader, I had a collection of children's classics, like the Estonian translations of *Little Lord Fauntleroy*, *Gulliver's Travels*, and *Adventures of Huckleberry Finn*, not to mention a series of books by Karl May about Indians and their Chief Winnetou. Therefore, I expected to find more books under the Christmas tree. Sure enough, I wasn't disappointed; there were several, all beautifully gift-wrapped. The most memorable one was titled *Teraspoiss* (*The Boy of Steel*). It was about a boy who stood up against a bully, winning the admiration of his classmates and even the respect of the bully himself.

There was also a surprise—an unusually huge, bulky package standing next to the Christmas tree. It turned out to be a small bookshelf. My mother was quick to explain: "Now you can keep all your books neatly in one place. I don't want to see them spread out all over the house anymore." It was an unmistakably clear message that she expected me to shape up in the coming year.

After the exchange of gifts, we sat down for a traditional Estonian Christmas dinner consisting of blood sausage, roasted pork, potatoes, and sauerkraut. The grown-ups enjoyed vodka and beer, while I drank a soft drink called *mõdu* from the local brewery. It looked like beer and made me feel very grown-up.

When I finally collapsed in bed, I was happy and content. It had been the best Christmas yet. I was proud to have my own library with many new additions and, most importantly, to be accepted and treated like a grown-up. I was no longer a child who believed in Santa Claus and got toys for Christmas. The future looked bright and promising. I fell asleep, blissfully unaware that my father would not be with us the next Christmas.

A year earlier, my father's friends had urged him to run for a seat in Riigivolikogu, the Lower House of the Parliament. My mother was not pleased with this idea. Her biggest worry was that he would have less time to spend with the family. She thought he had already taken on too many outside commitments, including Managing Director of Ephag—a publicly owned pharmaceutical company—and Chairman of the Chamber of Pharmacists. Despite her concerns, he decided to run, and was elected. Our family life changed just as my mother had predicted; he came home for dinner less frequently and often had to stay out late for evening meetings.

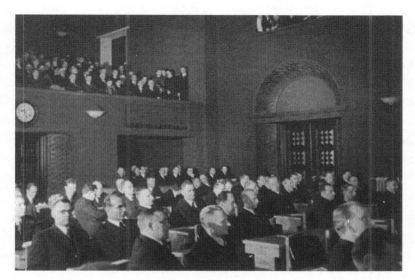

Riigivolikogu in session. My father is fourth man from the left in the second row

But there was also a bright side of his new position: besides his more important duties, he was expected to attend the Independence Day celebration. Better yet, I could go with him. Independence Day was observed on February 24, the date Estonia declared independence in 1918. The highlight of the day was a military parade at Vabaduse Väljak (Freedom Square). It was also the highlight of my childhood, because I hadn't yet seen anything bigger than a local firemen's parade. My mother bundled me up and off we went.

When we arrived, the viewing stand was surrounded by a sea of blue, black, and white Estonian flags. Clutching my father's hand, I followed him through the crowd to the reserved section in the front row for a close-up view of the action. He pointed out some important people on the reviewing stand: President Konstatin Päts and the head of the armed forces, General Johan Laidoner, whom I recognized from their portraits in my school's auditorium. The orchestra played the national anthem, and I sang proudly along with the crowd. The orchestra started again, this time with a triumphant military march. The officers came first, followed by the soldiers, who marched in precise military formation. I was so close to them that I could clearly see the insignia on the soldiers' uniforms and hear their thumping steps, which nearly muffled the marching band. Next came the cavalry officers, clad in colorful tunics, riding their horses in perfect formation. They were followed by fearsome artillery and motorized units. I was so mesmerized by the pomp and circumstance of the celebration that I didn't even notice the freezing weather. What a treat for an eight-year-old boy! Full of enthusiasm and excitement, I asked my father, "Can we do it again next year?"

"I hope so," he said in a wistful tone, as if he saw trouble looming.

As it turned out, the ebullient, full-scale parade celebrating the twenty-first birthday of the Estonian Republic in 1939 was the last one for my father and me. The next year's parade on Freedom Square was cancelled due to unexpected and dangerous geopolitical circumstances. And for the following five decades, the Estonian people were unable to publicly celebrate their much-revered Independence Day.

4

Paradise Lost

BY THE TIME the first rays of September sun reached my window, I was already wide awake after a restless night spent in anticipation. I had waited several weeks for this day. I was going to the airport and would get a close-up view of airplanes on the ground—a big day for a young boy who had seen airplanes only flying high in the sky.

It was Friday, September 1, 1939. My mother and I were going to send off my father to a conference in Berlin. Frankly, I was hoping that he would take me along with him. It would have been my first airplane flight and my first trip abroad, as well. But despite my pleadings, my father firmly rejected the idea. "This is a business trip for pharmacists," he said. "I will be busy in meetings every day. Wait until the next year when the Olympic Games will be held in Helsinki. Then we'll fly across the Gulf of Finland to watch the games. That's a promise."

I accepted his answer, knowing that my father always kept his word. Little did I know that this time he would not be able to keep his promise, because on that very day events were set in motion that changed the world. That was the day when World War II started. In the years that followed, millions of people were killed, cities and countries were destroyed, and countless lives were changed forever, including mine.

On the way to the airport, my father wanted to stop by his office to pick up some papers. The moment we entered the pharmacy, I noticed something strange. Instead of the usual subdued atmosphere, I saw several pharmacists huddled in agitated discussion behind the counter. The head pharmacist approached my father and asked, "Have you heard the news? It was just announced on the radio that the German Army has crossed the Polish border and is invading Poland. Germany is at war with Poland."

My mother looked worried. She turned to my father and asked, "Do you think it is wise to go to Germany now?"

"Wait here for a minute," he said. "I'll find out." He rushed to his office to call the conference organizers in Berlin. Unable to reach them, he returned and said, "Let's go to the airport and meet with the rest of the delegates. Then we can decide." He called a taxi, and off we went.

At Tallinn airport on the day when World War II began

At the airport we discovered that Lufthansa had cancelled all flights, but Finnair had a flight leaving for Berlin, and seats were still available. After a brief deliberation, the group of delegates decided to go. As they checked their baggage, I admired the shiny DC-3 on the tarmac, wishing that I could climb aboard and look at the cockpit. To my disappointment, that was not allowed, and I had to be content with posing for a photo in front of the aircraft. When it was time to board, my father said in a firm, assuring voice, "Don't worry, we will be safe." He kissed my mother, gave me a pat on the shoulder, and climbed on board. My mother held on to me as we waved and watched the plane roll toward the runway.

My father returned two days later. The conference had been cancelled, and he'd been stranded in Berlin until the next available flight back. Since he and his group were visiting Germany for the first time, they'd taken full advantage of the opportunity for sightseeing, souvenir-shopping, and sipping world-renowned German beer. I was most impressed by my father's description of the Berlin Zoo, where he had his photo taken with a tiger cub on his lap. Darned, I thought, I wish I could have been there. He brought home for me a genuine pair of *Lederhosen*, German leather shorts with a drop-front flap and fancy green suspenders. Still, I would have rather gone on the trip with him.

I remembered that first day of September as an exciting day at the airport. A war between two foreign countries seemed unimportant to an eight-year-old. However, the actions planned by two powerful dictators, Hitler and Stalin, would soon cruelly disrupt our lives and the lives of everyone living in Eastern Europe.

The seeds of this tragedy were actually sown a week earlier, on August 23, 1939, when the German Foreign Minister Joachim von Ribbentrop and his Soviet counterpart Vyacheslav Molotov raised glasses in Moscow to celebrate the signing of the German-Soviet Nonaggression Pact. With this document, they effectively redrew the entire map of the region. The pact included a secret protocol dividing the northern and eastern regions of Europe into German and Russian spheres of influence. This allowed Russia to occupy and annex the three Baltic States—Estonia, Latvia, and Lithuania. That pact was the beginning of our nightmare. My parents' aspirations and future plans were going to be destroyed in ways they never could have imagined, and my happy and carefree childhood would soon come to an unexpected end.

By the time my father returned from Berlin, Britain and France had declared war on Germany. Initially, the war had no noticeable impact on our lives. We were still far removed from the hostilities. The first time I noticed the war's effect was when oranges and bananas disappeared from the fruit bowl on our dining table. Shortly afterward, my parents began to worry about shortages of coffee and other imported goods.

I remember one afternoon when the doorbell rang and there was a man with a big, brown sack on his shoulder, asking, "Where shall I put it?" It turned to be a sack of sugar my father had bought in anticipation of a sugar shortage. The pantry was too crowded and the basement too damp for storing, so the sack ended up in my room, directly behind my bed. I didn't mind because I knew that there would be enough sugar to satisfy my sweet tooth for a long time to come.

Before long, discussions at the dinner table turned to the troubling actions of our next-door neighbor, Russia. Following the invasion of Poland, Stalin pressured Finland and the Baltic States to sign mutual-assistance treaties that would give Soviet Russia the right to establish military bases on our territories, allegedly for "our protection." With Soviet troops massed on the Estonian border, and without any help from the League of Nations, Great Britain, or the United States, Estonia had no choice but to acquiesce to the demands. The treaty was signed on September 28, 1939. Latvia and Lithuania signed similar treaties a few days later.

Finland, however, did not yield to Soviet demands and fought back a Soviet attack over a staged border incident. That started the Winter War, as it was called. It was particularly unsettling for us because it brought the fighting close to the Estonian border. I remember sitting with my father in his study, listening to daily radio reports from the front. We were pleased to learn how well the greatly outnumbered Finnish troops were able to hold off Soviet advances. The Finns used the agility of ski troops to their advantage and held fire until Soviet soldiers were close enough to make every bullet count. We cheered their battlefield victories and mourned their losses. The fighting ended the following spring, when Finland signed a peace treaty, giving up some territories but still maintaining its independence. In the meantime, we worried what would happen next.

By November 1939, Baltic Germans, many of whom had been living in Estonia for several generations, started to leave in response to Hitler's call for their return to Germany. The Benksons, who lived upstairs, were among the first to leave. My father's two partners at the pharmacy, Gustav Gnadeberg and Ewald Leyden, sold their shares to my father and joined the departing Germans. While my father was thrilled to have the pharmacy wholly under Estonian ownership, my mother considered it a sign of trouble to come. "This doesn't bode well," she said. "They must have had a reason for leaving. I think we'll see difficult times ahead."

Years later, my mother told me she had suggested moving to Sweden, a neutral country where my father had several business contacts who could have helped us. But he rejected the idea. His deep attachment to the pharmacy and his other commitments prevented him from leaving everything behind. He also told my mother that it would be irresponsible and cowardly for a member of parliament to leave the country at such a critical time.

On June 16, 1940, Soviet Russia demanded full access for additional troops throughout Estonia and the formation of a new Soviet-friendly government. Faced with overwhelming Soviet military force, and without any outside help, Estonia had no other choice but to yield to avoid bloodshed. The next day, masses of Soviet troops entered the country.

I will never forget that day. It started with a strange rumble that grew into a loud roar from the main road two blocks from our home. My mother and I went to investigate the source of that unusual noise. A convoy of Soviet armored vehicles and tanks was rolling down Vabaduse Puiestee (Freedom Boulevard). Having demonstrated its military might in the streets of Tallinn, it was now moving through our tranquil suburb of Nõmme. The unbearable noise was accompanied by a horrible smell of diesel fuel. On top of the crawling vehicles were strange-looking foreign soldiers with unfriendly faces, perspiring in their rumpled uniforms.

The onlookers on the sidewalk viewed the scene in solemn silence, like a group of mourners watching a funeral procession. Some tried to hide their tears behind handkerchiefs. The only time I saw someone smirk was when an armored car broke down and brought the entire convoy to a complete stop. I heard the disgruntled soldiers' voices, apparently swearing, as they struggled to repair the broken vehicle. Finally, my mother could no longer bear watching the disheartening scene and said, "I can't stand it anymore. Let's go home." We walked back slowly in silence. When we reached home, my mother broke down in tears.

Four days later, on June 21, communist-inspired demonstrations took place in front of the government offices. Backed by the Soviet tanks, the demonstrators called for the formation of a new government as dictated by the Soviet envoy, the mastermind of the takeover, Andrei Ždanov. The president was forced to replace his cabinet with new Soviet-friendly ministers.

Two weeks later, my father brought home the disturbing news that the newly appointed ministers had dissolved both houses of parliament. "They relieved us of all power and responsibilities," he said. "Now we are helpless bystanders in this tragedy."

"I was afraid of that," my mother said. "What's going to happen now?"

"New elections will be held in ten days. Some of the former members are planning to run again, to oppose the handpicked communist candidates. They are urging me to join them."

"Please don't," pleaded my mother. "That will be futile. The elections will be rigged. The communists won't let you win. You'll only become a target of their attacks. They're ruthless." After consulting with friends, my father finally decided not to file for his candidacy.

My mother was proven right. All candidates known for their patriotism and anti-communist views were disqualified as "enemies of the people." My father certainly would have been among them. When the election results were announced, we learned that all newly elected members belonged to the "Estonian Working People's Party." As my father read their names in the newspaper, he shook his head in disbelief and said, "I can't believe how many former socialists suddenly have become communists."

Six days after the election, on July 21, the new parliament met and, ignoring the Estonian constitution, voted to allow the Soviet Union to annex Estonia. On August 6, the Soviet masterminds behind the annexation in Moscow "accepted" the request. The takeover of Estonia by the Soviet Russia had become a *fait accompli*.

It was the sad end of a country that American author Marion Foster Washburn had discovered while writing her book, *A Search for a Happy Country*. According to her, Estonia, during its short years of independence, had succeeded in securing for its people the seven human necessities—food, shelter, work, health, education, freedom of expression, and love—without which no man or country can be happy.

Everyone sensed that our lives would be dramatically different under Soviet rule. "What will happen now?" I asked my mother.

"Life will be difficult," she said, recalling the days of Soviet occupation in Tartu two decades earlier. But even she couldn't imagine how much more difficult it would become.

5

Life Under the Red Flag

HIGH ON TOP of Toompea Hill, overlooking the city of Tallinn, is a thirteenth-century castle with a tall tower called Pikk Hermann (Tall Hermann). For centuries, the flag at its top had been the most visible symbol of the government in power. The sight of a red flag with yellow hammer and sickle, instead of the traditional Estonian blue, black, and white tricolor that had flown there for two decades, was a shocking introduction to a harsh new reality. I was too young to fully understand the significance of all that was happening, but I sensed from people around me that the country was no longer free.

The new regime wasted no time in imposing communist doctrine and Russian culture on us. Familiar programs on the state radio station were replaced with Soviet propaganda and Russian music. The music of Grieg and Sibelius was replaced by Tchaikovsky and Shostakovich; instead of jazz, we heard Russian ballads and balalaika music. I recall one particular song, "Katyusha," that was played repeatedly day after day. At first, I liked that catchy, melodious tune, but soon I tired of it, especially when I heard that it was a favorite song of the Russian soldiers.

Shortly after the takeover, a senior Russian naval officer and his family moved into the upstairs apartment left vacant by the Benksons. They had a son my age, Igor, who was quite friendly and eager to play with me. He taught me a few words of Russian, and I taught him some Estonian expressions in return. However, my parents made sure that we always maintained a cautious distance. The family appeared to be part of the Soviet elite, better educated and behaved than the uncivilized army troops who were seeing a modern, western lifestyle for the first time. I remember hearing stories about soldiers who tried to wash themselves in toilets, complaining, "The capitalist system is terrible. Each time you pull the chain, the water doesn't run long enough to finish washing." Another widespread story was about a soldier who bought a wrist watch and returned it the next day, accusing the store owner of selling him a defective watch. He calmed down only after he was shown how to rewind it.

The new government closed all private schools, including the English College that I had planned to attend in the fall. Therefore, I had to stay at my local school, which now had almost twice as many students as before due to the influx of former private-school students. To accommodate the overload, we attended classes in two shifts. I was assigned to the second shift, starting in the early afternoon and finishing after dark.

On the first day of school I immediately noticed several changes. We could no longer wear our colorful school caps—those were deemed by the new regime symbols of the former capitalist system. The auditorium had an entirely new look; all pictures in it had been replaced with portraits of Stalin and Lenin. There was no way of escaping their stern eyes staring at us from a sea of red flags and banners with communist slogans. During the opening assembly of the new school year, we no longer had our customary prayer. Instead, a speaker told us that Estonia had become part of "Great Mother Russia" and that we should be very happy about it. We had to sing "The Internationale," originally the battle hymn of French revolutionaries, which had become the official song of the Communist Party. Somehow, I could never understand who the oppressors were—whom were we supposed to overthrow? We had to sing a couple of more songs of praise for the Soviet Union, including one that began with the words "Big and wide is the country that is my home." Those propaganda sessions took place regularly every Monday throughout the school year, and attendance was mandatory.

Soon it became apparent that the goal of the new rulers was to seize and shape the minds of the young. Religious studies were abolished, and in history class we were lectured about the achievements of the Bolshevik revolution and the greatness of "Mother Russia." In foreign-language studies, which started in the fourth grade, Russian replaced German. As a third-grader, I was lucky to be spared. What amazed me most was how quickly the new rulers had managed to change and revise our textbooks. Even the math and science books had not escaped the scrutiny of the new editors, who inserted scattered references to Soviet Russian life into almost all textbooks.

Teachers encouraged us to create art and write articles for the bulletin board, where the best selections were to be displayed. It didn't take me long to discover that only those articles that praised communism were posted on the board. In search for recognition, I wrote a short piece about the benefits of socialist society. When I showed it to my mother, she was horrified. "This is terrible," she grumbled. "This is pure communist propaganda. Where did you learn this?"

"In history class," I explained. "The teacher told us that the new socialist system we have now is much better than our old capitalist society."

"Next time, when you want to write something for the bulletin board, please show it to me first," she said. "Don't believe everything they tell you in history class."

That was the end of my budding literary career. I never wrote another piece.

One day, when I returned to school after staying home sick, I was surprised to find a number of my classmates wearing white shirts and red scarves. They told me that a smooth-talking man had come to tell them about "Pioneers," an organization similar to the Boy Scouts and the Girl Scouts, but with a definite political agenda. He had painted a very attractive picture of the organization, emphasizing the recreational aspects of membership, while downplaying its political side.

Apparently, he had been quite convincing, considering the number of students who signed up on the spot. When I told my mother that I had missed the opportunity to join them, she said that I was lucky to be absent that day, and that I should say no to anyone trying to recruit me.

I was too young to fully understand the true nature of the Soviet regime, but it all unexpectedly became very clear on October 6, 1940, when my family's tranquil life was cruelly disrupted. The moment I woke up, I knew that something was wrong. My mother was standing by my bed, disheveled in her robe, and said, "Father didn't come home last night." That is odd, I thought. Father always came home, even if he had to attend meetings that lasted past midnight. What could have happened?

A phone call to his office failed to provide any clues. He had left the pharmacy at his usual time, and that was the last time anyone had seen him. As we were pondering all possibilities, the phone rang. My mother rushed to it, listened, said yes a couple of times, and hung up. "Who was that?" I asked.

"I don't know. A man said we should stay home and wait for the delivery man from the pharmacy." We thought that was odd because the pharmacy was temporarily without a delivery man. We were getting suspicious and started to fear the worst. We knew that people were being interrogated by the NKVD (the Soviet Secret Service, the forerunner of the infamous KGB) and wondered whether my father was also being detained for interrogation. So we waited, with mounting apprehension. My mother became increasingly nervous. Her hands began to tremble.

Suddenly, a large truck pulled up to our street corner and stopped, unable to turn into our narrow street. A couple of men came out, walked toward our house, and checked the house number. They said something to each other, returned to the vehicle, and tried to enter our street again. After several unsuccessful attempts, they left.

A while later, a black sedan pulled in front of our house. Four men came out and rang our doorbell. They identified themselves as members of NKVD and informed us that my father had been arrested the night before and that they had the authority to search our home. They asked everyone in the house to come forward to identify ourselves—that included my mother, my grandfather (who was living with us at the time), our maid, and me. We were ordered not to leave the house and to stay within sight of the agents.

"But my son has to eat and go to school in an hour," my mother protested. After a brief discussion among the agents, I was allowed to eat alone in the kitchen while one agent kept an eye on me. I still remember him with his dour look standing at the door, watching my every move. When it was time for me to leave, he searched my pockets and rummaged through my knapsack before letting me go.

With a heavy heart, I started to walk toward the school. I was afraid to tell anyone what had happened, except for my friend Heiki. He was the only classmate I could trust because he was in a similar situation as I was. His father had been arrested weeks earlier and he'd had no information about his whereabouts since. He was just as worried as I was. We tried to maintain our composure as we commiserated together during classroom breaks.

When I returned from school, I found our home in total disarray. The rooms behind the glass door—our living room, my parents' bedroom, and my room—had been sealed off. All clothing and other necessities that my mother had salvaged from those rooms were piled up in the hallway.

Pointing at the remaining rooms, my mother explained: "These will be our living quarters from now on. I had to let Vera go and Grandpa will go to her room. You will go to Grandpa's room, while I'll sleep in your father's study. Thank God they let us keep most of our furniture and belongings. The truck this morning probably was here to take away everything we owned. I have heard that they often confiscate the property of the arrested person's family." Then she described what had happened.

"They searched through our papers and books and took all photos of your father. Every group photo your father was in was taken. They also took all letters and postcards we had received from foreign countries. Then they made a complete inventory of items that re-mained behind the glass door and sealed the door—"

"But where is my father and when can I see him?" I interrupted her.

"He is in jail awaiting sentencing. We can't see him until then. That's all they told me. I'll try to contact some lawyers to see what they can do to get him released. Meanwhile, you have to be brave and pray for him every day."

A couple of weeks later, while I was at school, the agents returned to search our home again without explaining what they were looking for. However, they did find my father's rifle in the pantry and took it away. (As a member of the Defense League, my father had to keep a weapon at home so that he could be rapidly mobilized in case of national emergencies.) On their way out, they ordered my mother to report to their headquarters for further questioning the next evening.

Before my mother left, she tried to reassure me. "It's not a big deal. I'll be gone for a few hours," she said, but, at the same time, she began to prepare me for the possibility that she might not return. She showed me where she had hidden some cash and how to take care of Grandfather. "And remember, Aunt Elli lives only a few blocks away. You can always depend on her." Then, dressed in a plain outfit, she hugged and kissed me, and left for the appointment with the Devil.

That evening, I was more scared than ever before in my life. What if she doesn't return? I wondered. What will I do? How will I man-age, alone without parents in this world? As these fearful thoughts were racing through my mind, I prayed repeatedly, "Please God, let her return. And please bring my father back. Please God, let her re-turn," until I fell asleep.

It must have been around three or four in the morning when I was awakened by a tapping on my window. Words cannot describe the elation I felt when I saw my mother's face outside the window. Thank God, I thought, my mother is back. I will not be an orphan! She was waving for me to open the front door; she had intentionally left the key at home to keep it from falling into her interrogators' hands.

The moment she crossed the doorway, she reached for me and we hugged. I could feel her body trembling. "What happened?" I asked. She shook her head and looked at me in silence. Then she said, "Before they released me, I had to sign a statement promising not talk to anyone about the meeting."

All our attempts to get my father released through legal channels were unsuccessful. Meanwhile, life was getting worse daily. We lost our pharmacy—it was nationalized like other private businesses. Uncle Artur's pharmacy was seized in a similar fashion. Instead of letting him continue to work there, he was assigned to another pharmacy in the city. A few months later, he was reassigned to a different pharmacy out of town, requiring a lengthy commute by train, because his automobile had been taken away months earlier.

We had no Christmas cheer that winter. As part of the Sovietization campaign, all public Christmas celebrations were banned. There was no discussion of Christmas at school. It was replaced by *Nääripüha*, a celebration of winter and the beginning of the New Year. Instead of Christmas trees, we had New Year's trees, and Santa Claus was replaced by Father Frost. Still, most Estonians continued to celebrate Christmas secretly in their homes, and privately in their hearts.

It was particularly heartbreaking to observe Christmas without my father. We lit a couple of candles on the table and the four of us—my mother, Grandfather, Aunt Iti, and I— sang "Silent Night." After we had dried our eyes, we prayed the traditional Christmas prayer, and then we prayed for my father's health, and especially for the unlikely miracle that he might be released from prison before long.

That miracle did not happen. My father languished in jail until we were notified in April that he had been sentenced to eight years in Siberia as "a non-desirable element to communist society." We were then allowed to visit him to bring food and clothing. My mother wanted to see him first without me, afraid that the sight of him after several months in prison might leave me with a disturbing memory.

She did go alone, bringing him food and a letter I had written to him. She returned with a list of items my father needed. She told me that he wanted to see me before being sent away. I was happy that I was finally able to see him again. My mother collected and packed the things that he wanted and scheduled the prison appointment.

It was a cold, gloomy day when I left with my mother for the long-awaited meeting. We took a train to Tondi station, where we transferred to a streetcar that took us to the jail, a drab, gray building surrounded by a barbed-wire fence. My mother entered through a small side door, leaving me waiting outside. She returned a few minutes later with disappointment written all over her face. She put her arms around me and said gently, "I am afraid we can't see him. He is already on his way to Siberia." Then she looked toward the jail and said scornfully, "How cruel of them, letting us come, knowing that he had left already."

I found it hard to believe. How could they have done it? They had deprived me of the moment that I had desperately awaited for so long—to see my father and spend the last few moments with him before saying good-bye. Clutching my mother's hand, I walked back to the streetcar, disappointed and heartbroken.

When we got back home, my mother said, "I have something that your father wanted you to have. It's a letter that he wrote for you in prison." She handed me a small piece of something that looked like scrap paper, about four-by-six inches in size, with a message in my father's handwriting:

My dear son Jaak!

Since I must be away from home for a while then, please, my son, during that time, be a good son to your dear mother and help her in all matters and don't cause her any grief. Study diligently and grow up to be a big, fine and honest man, just like your father had always tried to be. I hug you and kiss you heartily.

Your loving Father

My father's letter from jail

I did not know what happened to my father until 1955, when I learned that he had survived the infamous Vorkuta Gulag prison camp and was released at the end of his sentence in 1948. He was not allowed to return to Estonia, but was sent to the Krasnoyarsk region, where he died in Tasseyevo on May 13, 1953. He must have had some satisfaction in knowing that he had outlived the person responsible for his suffering, his nemesis, Josef Stalin, who died two months before him on March 5.

After Estonia regained its independence and secret NKVD files became public, I was able to examine my father's file. The minutes of his interrogation revealed that the main charge against him was being a member of the Defense League. I also learned that he had been offered freedom on the condition that he would work for the NKVD as an informer. Asked why he refused the offer, he had replied, "Because of the brutal treatment I received during the interrogation."

6

The Web of Terror Widens

MY FATHER'S ARREST was a precursor to a wave of arrests that followed throughout the country. People disappeared more and more frequently. Although the primary targets were former government officials, scholars, professionals, and business owners, any well-to-do person— *kulak*, by Soviet definition—was in danger. All our friends lived in fear, not knowing who might be the next victim.

Aunt Senta's husband, Haakon Raudsepp, who was the Deputy Director of the National Audit Office (the equivalent of the Comptroller General in the United States), suspected that his freedom might be short-lived. His suspicion was confirmed when someone with information from a credible source warned him that his arrest was imminent. He had to decide fast what to do and where to go.

The borders had been closed since the government takeover. Only those able to claim some sort of German heritage were still allowed to leave the country. Most of those Baltic Germans had already left for Germany, but the few ships that were still departing were now full of fleeing Estonians who were able to prove their German ancestry. Many used forged documents in their desperation to save their lives.

After a frantic search, Uncle Haakon discovered a confirmation certificate from a German church he had belonged to in his youth. That document was sufficient to secure passage for his whole family. Leaving practically everything behind, he left on the next ship with his pregnant wife Senta and four-year-old son Andres. They departed as a family of three, but arrived in Gotenhafen as a family of four; Aunt Senta delivered a healthy baby daughter in the middle of the North Sea. She and the baby were taken off the ship on a stretcher and transported directly to a nearby hospital. At least they were out of immediate danger. How ironic that at a time when many people were fleeing from Nazi Germany, others found there safe haven from the tyranny of another dictator.

After my father's sentencing, we were allowed to enter the rooms that had been sealed off and reclaim our belongings. Still, we were not permitted to move back because another family had been assigned to occupy that part of our apartment. According to the Soviet rulers, our apartment was overly spacious for us, and therefore we had to relinquish half of our living space. That caused many new concerns and worries. How would we get by sharing one bathroom and a kitchen with another family? Who could these people be? Had they been ordered to spy on us and report everything we were doing?

Luckily, our new neighbors turned out to be a wonderful family— a young lawyer, Mr. Kallas, his wife, and their small baby. Having been forced out of their home, they were happy to find a new home with us. As I recall, we never had problems sharing the bathroom or the kitchen, nor did the baby's crying disturb us. My mother adored the baby and helped Mrs. Kallas with babysitting and advice. They became good friends and stayed in touch for many years after the war.

Because of the unsettling times following my father's arrest, my schoolwork suffered and I didn't make the honors list. I was disappointed, but when I saw one of the certificates, I was happily relieved that I didn't get one. In addition to the congratulatory message, the diplomas featured photos of Stalin and Lenin prominently above the student's name. It was a document from those responsible for my father's arrest that I could not possibly ever want to have.

The next calamity came on June 14, 1941. Recollections of that tragic day are etched into almost every Estonian's memory forever. For me, it started early in the morning with the ringing of the doorbell. To our surprise, we found Aunt Elli's maid, Miili, behind our door, visibly shaken and with tears in her eyes. "They took your sister away," she burst out. "And they took Mr. Puksov and the children too. The whole family."

"Who took them?" my mother asked.

"A bunch of men with rifles, some Russians in military uniforms, and some Estonians in civilian clothes. They said that the government had decided to send Estonians to new homes in Russia, where they are more needed than here. They allowed taking only as many things they could carry. They turned the house upside-down and took away all the jewelry and silverware they could find. 'You won't need them in your new home,' they said." She paused to wipe her tears, and continued, "They also said that many more families will be going with them, so I thought I should warn you. They might come after you, too."

My mother thanked her and immediately called Grandmother in Tartu, saying that Aunt Elli's family was being deported to Siberia and we may be next in line. Then she turned to me and said, "I am afraid that they might come and get us, too. I think we should start planning what to take with us so that we will be prepared when they come."

"Maybe we can go and hide," I suggested. "Somewhere where they can't find us."

"Where would we go?"

"Maybe Aunt Elli's house. They have been there already, so it might be safe."

"How long can we hide there? They will hunt us down eventually. I think it's better to be prepared and have our things packed before they come to get us. They only gave Aunt Elli an hour to pack."

I was surprised by how calmly my mother behaved, and how readily she accepted the possibility that we could be sent to Siberia. Years later, thinking back on that day, I believe that she may have harbored a secret hope of finding my father somewhere in a Siberian prison camp.

She brought out a rucksack and four suitcases—two large, and two small. Then she started to rummage through the closets and drawers, looking for the letter that my father had sent her from jail before he had been sent away. "In that letter," she said, "he had a list of items he wanted me to bring him before he left. That list is a good guide for what we'll need to survive in Siberia." The list turned out to be a harsh reminder of what kind of future we might face.

"Winter coat, felt boots, blankets, fur cap with ear flaps, woolen sweater, mittens . . ." my mother read from the list. "Although it's summer now, we'll need them later. Siberian winters can be terribly cold." She also took various necessities—soap, first-aid kit, sewing kit, pocket knife, writing paper, envelopes, and other small things— and tucked them around the bulky items in the suitcases.

We were finished by early afternoon. My mother, thinking that Grandfather would not be deported because of his age and poor health, prepared instructions for him and Aunt Iti on what to do in case the worst would happen to us. Then she made more than a few sandwiches; we ate some and packed the rest for the road. Then we began waiting for our captors, praying and hoping that they would never come. Despite my mother's attempt to look calm and brave, I could detect a sense of unusual nervousness. She paced the floor, back and forth, and occasionally peeked out of the front window. The street behind the pine trees appeared eerily quiet—there was not a soul in sight. The longer we waited without seeing a truck with armed soldiers, the more hopeful we became.

"Maybe we are lucky," I said to my mother. "Maybe they'll not take us after all." After sunset, we became more encouraged and started to breathe easier. Around midnight, we thought that we may have actually been spared and we went to bed.

The next morning we learned what really had happened. A country-wide deportation wave had uprooted thousands of families and packed them into cattle cars at various train stations. The victims from our area were held on a train in Pääsküla, only a couple of miles from us.

Meanwhile, Grandmother arrived from Tartu, hoping to find her daughter Elli on the train so that she might say goodbye. She was heartbroken. She kept sobbing and repeating over and over again, "Why did they take them? Why them? They had done nothing. They were never involved in politics." It was very hard for her. Having already lost a son-in-law, she was now grieving the loss of another son-in-law, her favorite daughter, and grandchildren.

We packed a few items of clothing, food, and water and left for the train station, hoping to see Aunt Elli before the train left. When we arrived, we saw a long train of cattle cars full of people, surrounded by soldiers with rifles who blocked anyone attempting to approach it. We walked along the phalanx of guards while my mother and Grandmother repeatedly shouted Aunt Elli's name. All we could hear were babies crying and people calling the names of their loved ones, hoping to make contact. Despite our efforts, there was no response from Aunt Elli. We stood in the hot sun, helplessly observing the tragedy unfolding in front of our eyes.

As we watched in horror, more victims were brought in on small trucks and herded into the cars. I noticed that men were separated from their families and loaded into separate cars. There was a mother desperately trying to keep her toddlers together as she ushered them onto the train. One crying woman appeared to be pregnant and yet another was holding a small infant in her arms. How, I wondered, can anyone be so cruel as to afflict so much suffering on innocent people? How will they survive such inhuman treatment? I could never forget this painful scene—it haunted me for many days and nights afterward.

Our attempts to find Aunt Elli had been futile and we walked home, exhausted and heartbroken. As we passed the house of my friend Heiki, I learned that his home had been ransacked and that he, his mother, and sister had also been deported. I had lost my best friend and all my close relatives in a single day.

The trains left the following day, destination unknown. We only knew that they were heading towards some faraway place in Siberia, where my father and many other Estonian men were held in prison camps.

Years later, I learned that Aunt Elli and her children, Eda and Ilmar, were sent to work in a *kolkhoz* (a Soviet collective farm) in Kirov Oblast, about a thousand kilometers northeast of Moscow, where "enemies of the people" were being resettled by the tens of thousands. Her husband, Uncle Artur, landed in a gulag in the Northern Ural Mountains, where he was one of the first prisoners to die from the inhumane working conditions. Eda and Ilmar were allowed to return to their home in 1946. Four years later, they were arrested again and deported back to Siberia because, after reaching adulthood, they had become "politically dangerous" to the Soviet government. Eventually, they were able to reunite with their mother back in Estonia in 1961.

My mother's cousin, Hilda Rass, whose husband had been arrested and shot shortly after the Soviet takeover, was also deported with her two children. Pregnant with her third child at the time, she gave birth to a son six months later in Siberia. Two years after that, she died from working under harsh conditions and a lack of medical care. All of her three children were placed in an orphanage. Her first husband, the father of her oldest child, Monika, had luckily escaped deportation. As a lawyer, he somehow was able to locate Monika through the Soviet bureaucracy and bring her back home. When she refused to go home without her two younger half-brothers, he took them back as well.

They were lucky survivors because less than half of the deported returned to their homeland. By and large, these were women and their children who had grown up in internment. Very few men returned— most of them were shot or perished during their first year in the harsh Siberian winter.

Over 10,000 Estonians were deported in that dreadful raid of June 14. It was a huge loss for a small country, comparable to losing the population of the state of Iowa in the United States. Similar deportations were carried out simultaneously in the other two Baltic countries, Latvia and Lithuania. According to documents discovered later, additional deportations had been planned to follow; my mother and I were on the list for the next raid. Luckily for us, the perpetrators were unable to carry out their evil plans. A week after the June raid, Soviet soldiers were busy fighting the German Wehrmacht.

7

The Germans are Coming

O N JUNE 22, 1941, during a Sunday afternoon walk with my mother, we met a couple of neighbors chatting on our street corner. They appeared excited, more spirited than we had seen them for a long time.

"Have you heard the good news?" they shouted. "Germany attacked Russia this morning."

"My God!" My mother beamed. "I can't believe it. This is fantastic news."

"We heard the Germans are advancing rapidly. If it's another blitzkrieg, then they'll be here in no time."

"I hope so, but I wish they had the started the war sooner," my mother remarked wistfully. "Aunt Elli would have been still here." After a moment of silence, she looked up and added, "But, better late than never."

At last, an end to the painful suffering under Soviet occupation was in sight. We continued to walk home with a bounce in our stride and hearts full of hope.

Information about the war was sketchy. Newspapers featured stories about the bravery of Russian soldiers, but offered no clues as to where the fighting was taking place. Rumors circulated that the German Army had broken through Russian defenses and was advancing north, in our direction. We were unable to get any news from foreign

radio stations because all radio receivers had been confiscated immediately after the invasion started. I remember lugging our huge radio
console to my schoolhouse where radios were collected and stored.
We really didn't regret giving it up because it had stopped working
anyway.

The Soviet naval officer and his family living above us left suddenly without saying a word. We weren't surprised, since they had
stopped talking to us immediately after my father's arrest. A young
minister and his wife moved to the vacated apartment shortly thereafter.

All draft-age men were ordered to be conscripted into the Soviet
Army. The order was received with a great deal of suspicion. Was it
another deportation to Siberia in disguise, or would the men be used
as cannon fodder in the fight against the Germans? Anticipating a
speedy arrival of German troops, many men ignored the order and
went into hiding or found other ways to evade the draft. Others fled
into the forests, where they formed organized cells of resistance, col-
lectively known as the "Forest Brothers," against the Soviet Army.

Women were conscripted to dig fortifications for anticipated
battles at the outer reaches of Tallinn. My mother, too, received orders to join one of these work units. That meant she would have to be
away from home for a week—or even longer.

"I don't know how much good I can do for them, but I'm afraid to
ignore the order," she said. She explained to me how to take care of
Grandfather, who was getting on in age. She also told me where to
buy food and gave me elementary cooking lessons. Then she packed
her rucksack and left, putting me, at the tender age of ten, in charge of
the household.

Every morning, I went to the corner food store and bought two
fresh French rolls to go with hard-boiled eggs for breakfast. I prepared the eggs on a kerosene-burning Primus stove precisely according to my mother's instruction. Midday dinner presented a real test of
my culinary skills. I harvested string beans from our garden, cooked
and served them with pan-browned butter and boiled red potatoes.
Any vegetarian would have loved it. Dessert came from the garden as

well; we had raspberries and a choice of three types of currants—red, white, and black. A simple supper of sliced salami and cheese with dark Estonian rye bread was a breeze to prepare. To my surprise, I enjoyed being a chef, but I was not so keen on cleaning up and washing dishes.

I loved to take care of Grandfather and enjoyed his company at the kitchen table, where we ate our meals. Even though he had been with us for more than a year, that was the first time I really got to know him. He was a modest, wise old man, who loved to share his wisdom with me, always in an unassuming, nonjudgmental way. Our conversations covered a wide range of topics. He talked affectionately about his marriage to Grandmother, how they had raised their children, and how proud he was of my father's accomplishments. It was so relaxing to be with him that I felt comfortable confiding my innermost thoughts and concerns. Those memorable days with Grandfather brought us closer than we had ever been before.

Fortunately, my mother didn't have to suffer the hardship and indignity of digging trenches for long. When a father's friend heard about her situation, he got her transferred to a high-priority project at the pharmaceutical firm Ephag, making improvised gas masks for the Soviet Army. It involved assembling layers of specially impregnated gauzes into face masks in a clean, pleasant laboratory environment. Thanks to that friend, my mother was rescued from backbreaking outdoor labor.

I was just as happy as my mother to have her back from her grueling ordeal. When she walked through the front door, she was hardly recognizable—her sunburned face was dark as chocolate under her dust-covered hair. Though she was dirty and exhausted, she was in high spirits. "It was hard work, but whenever the guards were not looking, we stopped and just chatted," she chuckled. "I don't think those trenches will do the Russians any good against the well-armed German troops."

My mother was right. The German Army moved at a fast pace and reached Estonian territory by early July, but then the advance stalled just short of reaching the city of Tartu. My mother was becoming increasingly concerned about Grandmother's safety, since all lines of communication were cut off, and we heard rumors about heavy fighting in Tartu.

We had to wait almost a month before we began to hear the sound of artillery fire. It was a clear sign that the front line was getting close. As the rumble grew louder, we started to plan for the likelihood of getting caught in the midst of the fighting armies. We were also afraid of the "Destruction Battalions," the paramilitary units of devoted communists who'd pledged to carry out Stalin's scorched-earth policy of destroying everything left behind by retreating Soviet troops. My mother, who had experienced military conflict in the First World War, decided to create a safe hiding place in our basement. I remember helping her carry mattresses, blankets, pillows, and food supplies downstairs in preparation for the forthcoming battle.

That moment came sooner than we expected. A series of bomb attacks by the German Luftwaffe, followed by blasts of artillery fire, confirmed that it was time to take shelter downstairs. Mrs. Kallas and her baby joined us. She explained that her husband was recovering from an appendectomy in the nearby hospital. It certainly was an interesting coincidence that his appendicitis attack occurred just when he was supposed to be conscripted. The young minister's wife from the upstairs apartment also came down, carrying a mattress under which she planned to hide her draft-age husband, should anyone come looking for him.

The sounds of artillery fire and bomb blasts came from all directions and lasted throughout the night. We felt relatively safe in our candlelit basement until a booming explosion shook our house and shattered the basement window. Minutes later, we smelled smoke and saw a faint orange glow behind the broken window.

My mother and I ran out to discover that the house behind our backyard was on fire. A bucket brigade of neighbors was frantically trying to extinguish the flames coming out of the windows. We became worried that these flames might ignite the pine trees next to the burning house, spread to the trees in our yard, and eventually reach our house. The danger of getting hit by artillery shells was suddenly replaced by the threat of losing our home to fire.

Filled with fear, we stood outside and watched two old men furiously work with axes and saws to cut down the threatened trees. Only after the trees had been felled, and the fire brought under control, did we breathe easily again. By that time the gunfire had ceased, leaving only the crackling sound of small-arms fire in the air.

By daybreak, everything seemed eerily quiet. We climbed out of the basement and heard from the people on the street that German troops had taken control of Tallinn. The Soviet military had been busy evacuating communist leaders and their own troops rather than fighting the advancing German forces. It was August 28, 1941, thirty-six days from the beginning of the invasion. When a neighbor said that the blue, black, and white tricolor of Estonia had been raised on top of the Tall Hermann tower, everybody cheered. A painful period in our lives appeared to be over.

In the attempt to get our lives back in order, Grandfather managed to hurt himself when he came upstairs and tried to sit on his bed, unaware that the mattress was still in the basement. He lost his balance and fell against the bed frame, which left a bloody gash on the back of his head. What an irony, surviving the dangers of the battle and getting injured when the fighting was over.

Mr. Kallas arrived unexpectedly from the hospital, looking perfectly healthy. He grinned and said that he didn't need an appendectomy after all; his doctor had performed a fake surgery only to save him from being drafted into the Soviet Army.

Later in the day, we could hear troop movements on Vabaduse Puiestee. I could not resist my curiosity and rushed out to see our liberators. The sight of the soldiers in neat green-gray uniforms, marching in unison and singing a song about a flower called Erika, was a refreshing change from the uncivilized Soviet soldiers. And the officers on motorcycles with sidecars racing alongside the marching troops made the picture of the victorious army complete.

A few days later, Grandmother arrived from Tartu. We were elated to see her standing at the front door, safe and sound. But our joy turned to grief when we heard her story.

"When the fighting was getting close to Tartu," she said, "Russian soldiers came and took my hotel. They had rifles and said they needed it for the soldiers. They just kicked us out. My staff and all my guests, everyone had to leave."

"And where did you go?" my mother asked.

"I took a few things and went to Karli's farm to stay out of danger. When the Germans came and the fighting was over, Karli took me back to Tartu." Grandmother started to sob. "My hotel was gone. The Russians had burned it down, almost down to the foundation. They even blew up the beautiful Stone Bridge."

"My God! That is unbelievable," my mother gasped. "They really are wild animals. I remember when Stalin said he would leave everything burning for the Germans, but I didn't believe that they would actually do it."

Grandmother was devastated. "All my belongings are gone—my clothes, my books, the family photos, all my treasures. What I miss most are my looms and the carpet designs. How can I replace them? And how am I going to survive? I have no income anymore."

"Don't worry," my mother assured her. "Karli and I will take care of you." She embraced Grandmother, brushed her hair aside, and kissed her tear-moistened cheeks.

It was heartbreaking to hear Grandmother's tragic story of losing her home and beloved hotel. I couldn't help but think of my visits to her gracious home, where I had spent many happy days with her. I was sad that this wonderful woman, who had already suffered so much during the Russian occupation, had to experience more misfortune and grief. She certainly didn't deserve it. The best thing we could do now was to provide her with shelter, and to try to put our lives together under the new rulers.

8

Life under German Occupation

A T FIRST, THE arrival OF German troops was greeted with immense relief and joy. We felt liberated from the tyranny of Soviet occupation, and we hoped that the Germans might restore our pre-war independence. That illusion, however, was quickly dashed when the Estonian tricolor on top of Big Hermann was swiftly replaced by the swastika flag of the Third Reich. All three Baltic countries became a single German-occupied territory, called Ostland. That meant another occupation under a different regime. A puppet government under the control of German military leadership was established; the city of Tallinn was renamed Reval, and Tartu became Dorpat, according to their medieval Germanic names.

The Estonian economy was in a shambles in the aftermath of the fighting. We were without electricity for months because Soviet destruction battalions had blown up the city's electric power station. Everything after sunset was done by the light of candles and kerosene lamps. Dining by candlelight was no longer considered romantic under these circumstances. We had to boil all our drinking water because Lake Ülemiste, the main source of our water supply, had been contaminated with the corpses of Russian soldiers. Local farm products were destined for the Wehrmacht and the civilian population in Germany, while Estonians were left to struggle with shortages that quickly led to food rationing.

In contrast to the Soviets, however, the German occupiers allowed considerable cultural autonomy. The radios that had been confiscated by the Russians were returned to their owners. But listening to foreign radio stations outside German-controlled regions was prohibited. When we brought our radio home, we were pleasantly surprised to find it back in working condition; the problem had been, most likely, a loose connection.

At school, all traces of Soviet influence were eliminated and teaching was conducted for the most part as in the pre-war days of independence. Monday-morning prayer sessions were reinstated, and German replaced Russian as the foreign language. History, however, was taught now from the perspective of the Third Reich.

We gave up our apartment and, together with my grandparents, moved into Aunt Elli's house. My mother became the official care-taker of the property. It was a big, two-story house with a huge yard full of pine trees and several apple trees. It even had its own private water well, which we hoped would be a source of pure drinking water. Unfortunately, the well turned out to be useless because we were unable to operate the water pump without electricity. As a result, I ended up hauling bucketfuls of water from the next-door neighbor every morning until electric power was restored.

We stored most of Aunt Elli's furniture and belongings in the garage and attic to make room for our own. We kept her upright piano in the living room because it was too difficult to move. My mother hoped that its presence might spark my interest in playing, but she soon discovered that I had little interest and even less talent for it. So the piano remained in its place to adorn our living room and collect dust.

I was far more interested in Aunt Elli's dog. Miku was a white spitz with spiked ears and a curly tail. At first, he pined for his former owners, but soon he turned into a good companion of mine. He followed me everywhere I went, even to school on some days. Before long, Miku became my sole responsibility; I made sure that he was properly fed and taken care of.

Soon after the German takeover, Uncle Haakon returned from Germany to assume a position comparable to the one he had formerly held in the National Audit Office. He moved in with us until he could arrange for his family—Aunt Senta and their children—to join him.

Uncle Haakon also helped us start the complicated process of getting back our pharmacy, which had been seized by the Soviets. He and my mother became its legal caretakers, and she began to work there as the cashier. In that position, she was able to earn an income and, perhaps more importantly, keep an eye on the firm's revenues. An added benefit was access to pure alcohol—a real lifesaver—which she could bring home without a doctor's prescription. Officially, it was intended for medicinal purposes, but we used it to buy food on the black market and thus supplement our meager rations. Although trading on the black market was illegal and punishable by stiff penalties—being executed on the spot, or sent to concentration camps—we could still buy scarce foods, such as ham and butter, from trusted suppliers.

The first winter under German occupation was exceptionally cold and harsh. At the start of the season, we sealed off all windows with insulation to protect us from winter's chill. Only one window was left unsealed for occasional airing of the rooms. As the temperatures dropped, we closed off the rooms on the first floor, moved upstairs, and heated only the upstairs living space, to conserve firewood and briquettes. I still remember how I hated the morning ritual: stepping out of bed into the ice-cold room, wrapped in blankets, and clinging to the ceramic furnace in search of whatever warmth remained from the previous evening's fire.

Schools were often closed for days at a time because of frigid weather. When we did have classes, we wore overcoats and gloves in the barely heated classrooms. But even gloves couldn't protect my fingers from developing the painful swelling and itching of chilblains.

I remember Christmas of that year as another sad one. In the afternoon of Christmas Eve, I went with my mother and Aunt Iti to visit Grandfather in the hospital. He was suffering from gangrene, and because he had refused to have his leg amputated, the doctors did not expect him to live much longer. We brought along a few gifts and wished him a Merry Christmas, knowing that it would be his last. However, we didn't realize that it was also the last time we would see him.

We had barely returned home and sat down for the Christmas Eve dinner when the phone rang, and we were informed that Grandfather had just passed away. Stunned and saddened by the news, we prayed and sat in silence for a long time. We tried to sing "Silent Night," but the joy of Christmas was not there. It was a somber Christmas Eve—after having already lost so many members of our family, we had just lost another.

For me, the loss meant more than that; I had lost my dear friend and a trusted companion. It was barely six months ago when, in my mother's absence, Grandfather and I had developed a special friendship. I cooked for him, we dined together and enjoyed, interesting and stimulating discussions. We continued those conversations after we moved to Aunt Elli's house. I remember sitting in the corner of her garden, soaking up the warm rays of the morning sun, trying to make sense of the world around us. Grandfather was the best storyteller, and a good listener as well. I wondered who else would sit there now to share my thoughts or give advice.

Fortunately, Uncle Haakon was there to fill that void. Since his return from Germany, he had become a father substitute who provided much needed male companionship for me. I could always turn to him when I needed advice or a helping hand. When the snow melted and spring arrived, we would go for long walks in the nearby pine forests, where we often discovered all sorts of military equipment that had been abandoned by the retreating Soviet Army. One day we came home with a steel helmet, small-arms ammunition, and two defused hand grenades. My mother was horrified. I had to keep them hidden in the backyard because she wouldn't allow me to bring them into the house. But what really upset her was the Russian Nagant revolver that I brought home a week later. She had good reason to be concerned because we certainly would have been arrested had the Gestapo found it. So I hid it in a secret place where no one, not even my mother, could find it.

When the threat of Soviet air raids became more apparent, Uncle Haakon designed a dugout shelter that he and I built in the backyard. We first dug a Z-shaped trench, then covered and reinforced it with logs and sandbags, leaving openings for access at each end. Though it couldn't protect us from a direct bomb hit, it was good enough to shield us from flying shrapnel. It was also safer than the basement if our house collapsed. In case of nearby bomb blasts, we applied tape in a criss-crossed pattern on all the windows, to prevent the glass from shattering. For fighting fires caused by incendiary bombs, we kept a box of sand and a couple of shovels in the attic and went to Nõmme market square, where the local fire department demonstrated proper ways of extinguishing those fires.

Eventually, Aunt Senta was permitted to return, and Uncle Haakon went to Germany to bring the family home. They moved upstairs, while my mother and I stayed downstairs. It was pure joy to see them after more than a year of absence. We were delighted to see that Cousin Andres had grown into a delightful five-year-old boy. However, the real attention-getter was his sister, the beautiful baby born in the middle of the Baltic Sea, whom we were meeting for the first time. Almost two years old, she was overdue for her baptism, which had been delayed until the family could return to Estonia. Soon after her arrival, she was christened Marike by our family minister in the upstairs living room with a small group of family and friends present. She was the star of the show during the ceremony. As the minister was about to drop water on her forehead, she admonished him by whispering, "Don't do it."

As German positions on the Eastern front started to deteriorate, efforts to recruit Estonian men into the German Army intensified. When the number of volunteers failed to meet expectations, a general mobilization was called.

When I arrived at school one morning, we were informed that one of our draft-age teachers was no longer with the school. Without any explanation, another teacher took over his class. All the students wondered what had happened.

Uncle Haakon and Aunt Senta with Andres and
Marike in 1943

"He joined the Finnish Boys," a well-informed classmate whispered into my ear. I knew exactly what he meant. Finnish Boys were men unwilling to fight in the German uniform. Instead, they fled to Finland to join the battle against the Soviets in the Finnish Army. It was relatively easy to evade German border guards and reach Finland by skiing across the frozen Gulf of Finland, where the total number of Finnish Boys had reached about 3,500.

We discovered the dark side of the Nazi regime when we heard that a Jewish family on our street had suddenly disappeared without a trace. We had no idea what had happened to them. We wondered whether they went into hiding or were rounded up by the Gestapo. Did they finally perish in some concentration camp, like many other Jewish families in the occupied territories, or did they survive?

Everyday life during the German occupation was rather bleak. Although the fear of being deported to Siberia was gone, we lived under somber wartime conditions. The city of Leningrad, under siege by German forces, was less than 200 miles away, and Estonian cities were still within the reach of Soviet bombers. Every time we looked out the window, criss-crossed reinforcing tape on the glass reminded us of the ever-present air raid threat. At night, the neighborhood was pitch-black because of a strictly enforced blackout. Everyone wore phosphor-illuminated buttons to avoid bumping into others on the street. Only on moonlit nights, when snow blanketed the ground, could we walk without those buttons. But those were the nights when we most worried about the increased threat of Soviet bombers.

As time went by, food shortages became more widespread. I remember many occasions when meat was not available and we had to accept fish as a substitute. My mother's resourcefulness helped us get cod liver oil from the pharmacy to supplement my nutritional needs. Despite my repeated protests, she made me swallow that terrible stuff every morning, until I finally accepted it as a necessary nuisance.

When the already dismal food situation in the cities worsened, we became more dependent on supplies from Uncle Karli's farm, brought by Grandmother whenever she came for a visit. She always apologized for not bringing more food; had she carried larger packages, she would have drawn police attention as a suspected black marketer. Each time she came, we feasted on bacon, ham, and fresh eggs—all the things we had not seen for a while. I am not sure whether I was more thankful for her presence or for the foodstuffs she brought with her.

As soon as school was out for the summer, I was sent to Uncle Karli's farm to be properly nourished and safe from the threat of air raids. Although I missed my friends and Miku back home, I found living on the farm thoroughly enjoyable. Each day was a new adventure, filled with many surprises and discoveries. I loved animals and the farm had plenty of them: a dozen cows, four horses, many pigs, chickens, geese, and turkeys.

Horses were my favorites. Uncle Karli considered horseback riding too dangerous for me and had forbidden it. But occasionally, when he was not around, I persuaded Stephan, the Russian prisoner of war assigned to work on the farm, to let me climb on a horse and ride around the field. It was a thrilling experience that remained a secret between us. Stephan was an intelligent young man from the Ukraine, conscripted into the Russian army and captured by the German troops. Tall and muscular, he worked tirelessly and made friends easily. Uncle Karli treated him with the same respect as he treated other workers. Stephan and I got along splendidly. I helped him improve his limited command of Estonian; he gave me Russian lessons in return. My other favorite summer pastimes included wandering through the woods, picking wild strawberries, and catching small fish in the local river.

Uncle Karli and his rye harvest

Life on a farm was a great learning experience for a sheltered boy from the city. I discovered how crops were harvested and processed before the final product reached our dinner table. I watched the milk-maids milk the cows and saw how they made cheese and butter. Uncle Karli encouraged me to give a hand to the workers, as long as I could do the job. So I tried almost everything, but my typical chores were herding cattle, helping men harness horses, and stacking hay. I worked with men and women, just like everyone else, except that I had the choice of quitting whenever I got bored or tired.

The farm workers spoke a southern dialect which was different from the language spoken in Tallinn. Not only did they pronounce words differently, but they used words that were totally new to me. In my attempt to fit in, I tried to use as many colloquial expressions as possible in conversations. I even picked up a few questionable words from the workers in the field that led to some embarrassing moments when I used them at the dinner table with Uncle Karli and Aunt Olli.

Foul language was not the only vice I picked up on the farm. During my second summer, the boy whom I had occasionally helped herd the cattle showed me a small shed behind the barn where Uncle Karli dried and cured tobacco leaves. The dark yellow leaves were hung on strings like laundry on a clothesline. My friend grabbed one of those leaves and cut it into thin shreds from which he rolled a makeshift cigarette. He lighted it with a match and took a couple of puffs. "Try it," he said and handed it to me. The first couple of puffs tasted horrible and made me cough. The next puffs were more agreeable, and we decided to repeat our secret adventure later in the week.

When we met again, my "partner in crime" brought with him a real cigarette. What a treat! Smoking the real thing, we felt incredibly important, tapping the cigarette as grown-up men did to discard ashes from the tip of the cigarette. I certainly thought I had made a major step toward manhood. Later on, we took up pipe-smoking because it was more practical than rolling cigarettes, which were always falling apart. Each of us had our own pipe; I kept mine carefully hidden in a suitcase next to my tobacco pouch, hoping that Uncle Karli wouldn't find it. Fortunately, he never did. My new hobby came to an unexpected end when I returned home in the fall. It ended before I could run out of tobacco or lose my southern accent. It ended when my mother found my pipe and threw it away.

Aside from the pipe incident, my mother was pleased that I had grown and gained weight during the summer. But she found it hard to accept that I was no longer the small boy who had left; I was almost a teenager, with a mind of my own. It was not easy for me to make the adjustment from an independent, carefree life in the country back to the dreary routine at home, where food rationing and bomb threats were commonplace.

To find solace in these difficult times, our family often turned to music. On the local radio station we heard Bach and Beethoven, but no more Tchaikovsky and Shostakovich. Hitler's favorite composer, Richard Wagner, was also featured from time to time. I found it boring and listened to lighter music that was broadcasted to lift the spirits of the military troops and the civilian population alike. I remember one particular song, "Lili Marleen," sung by Lale Andersen, which took the Estonian public by storm. When the war was over, I discovered that it was equally appreciated by soldiers on all sides of the battle. Another German *Schlager* (popular song) that hit a responsive chord in everyone's heart was *"Es geht alles vorüber, es geht alles vorbei."* An English language version of it would go like this:

"They say everything passes, everything passes away / But after December, comes always a May."

My mother and Aunt Senta were forever singing this catchy waltz tune, hoping the war would end soon and our living conditions would improve. But the war went on without an end in sight. Estonia, like every occupied country, was not a happy place. Dancing was banned in public places because it was considered too frivolous while men were fighting on the front. The only opportunities for entertainment were the movies.

The son of the local movie theater happened to be my classmate and a good friend. He was able to get movie tickets for his friends just by calling the box office. This allowed us to walk in at the last minute and bypass the ticket line. Furthermore, we could sit in the adults-only balcony, while other schoolboys had to bend back their necks while watching the film from the orchestra. Though we didn't always fully understand German-language films, we enjoyed them anyway, and learned some German as well. The weekly newsreels, *Die Deutsche Wochenschauen*, which preceded the feature films, were always of interest to us, particularly the part containing news from the Russian front.

Traveling in those years was not easy. Local commuter trains to Tallinn were always overcrowded. To avoid being trampled by fellow passengers in stifling compartments, my friends and I preferred to travel standing on the outside running board. But we could only do it when the weather was good and when the police were not watching.

Long-distance travel was restricted because the trains were used mostly for military transport. Travel permits were issued only to civilians who could present a valid reason for travel. The only time I was able to travel beyond Tallinn was when I went to spend summers on Uncle Karli's farm.

I couldn't have been more excited when my mother came home one spring evening and announced that she was going on a day trip to Aegviidu. "It's a small town in the countryside, approximately fifty-five kilometers from here," she said. "I'm going with my coworkers from the pharmacy to collect some herbs in a nearby forest. That is the official reason, so that we can get travel permits. But the real purpose is to get a break from the tedium of everyday work and have some fun."

"That's wonderful," I said. "Can I go, too?"

"Of course, you've just turned thirteen and are old enough now. But there is only one problem: the list of travelers has been already submitted. You can't get a train ticket without a permit." After thinking for a moment, she added, "But there is always someone who may not show up, and then you could take his place. Let's go and see what happens."

So we did go. At the train station we discovered that everyone on the list had shown up. We had to decide whether I should go or stay behind. The group leader resolved our dilemma by suggesting, "Why don't you come along and stay close to the group? I will keep all the tickets and show them all together to the conductor. The train will be so crowded that he won't even notice an extra person."

He was right. The train of several freight cars was jam-packed with passengers, like sardines in a can. That's perfect, I thought. I'll get easily lost in the crowd. When the conductor came on board, everything seemed to go according to plan. Our group leader showed him a bundle of tickets and pointed to our group. I was holding my breath and my heart was racing. The conductor glanced at us, nodded his head, and moved on to the next passenger. Our scheme had worked. What a relief!

Unfortunately, my joy didn't last long. At the next station, the moment the conductor left, two men sneaked on board from the opposite side of the platform. The conductor noticed them and returned.

"The two men who just came on board," he shouted. "I need to check your tickets. Please come forward."

When they failed to do so, he started to recheck each passenger's ticket individually. My heart fell. This time there would be no escape. Our fast-thinking group leader, however, found a way to keep us away from the conductor's inquisitive eyes. He stepped toward the conductor, pointed at the stowaways, and said, "These two men came on board." I felt an immense sense of relief when I saw the conductor apprehend the culprits and take them away at the next station. I was lucky again. Our group leader was the hero of the day and my mother and I couldn't thank him enough for his fast action. "That was the only way to save you," he explained his decision. "The men would have been caught anyway."

We got off the train at Aegviidu and spent a delightful day in the country. I enjoyed the fresh air, the smell of wildflowers, and a bountiful picnic catered by local farmers. In the evening, I even heard a nightingale sing. I knew about the mystical nightingale from poems and songs, but had never heard its beautiful sound before.

On the return trip we traveled in total darkness with a group of German soldiers at the opposite end of a half-empty cattle car. They sang and drank until they finally fell asleep. No one came to check our tickets. It had been an exciting day.

9

Red Army at the Doorstep

A S TIME WENT on, life became more and more difficult and unsettling. News from the front was disheartening. At the beginning of February 1944, we learned that Soviet troops had reached the Estonian border and threatened to enter Estonian territory. Another mobilization call for men into military service was issued. This time it was more successful than the previous one. Young men were concerned about the looming threat of a new Soviet occupation and wanted to help fend it off until Germany surrendered to the Western Allies. They hoped for the eventual restoration of Estonian independence and considered fighting for the homeland a moral duty, regardless of what country's uniform they wore. The new fighters were consolidated with previous conscripts and volunteers into an all-Estonian combat division, known as the Estonian Legion.

The nearness of the front became palpable to me when my school building was taken over by the Wehrmacht and converted to a military hospital. I remember watching military vehicles with Red Cross markings entering and leaving the closely guarded gate, presumably delivering wounded soldiers. Our classes were moved to various public buildings; mine were held in a crowded clubhouse in Hiiu, about a mile and a half from my home. Occasionally, we experienced Soviet air raids, which were directed mostly at military supply lines. Therefore, we considered ourselves to be relatively safe living in a residential suburban neighborhood.

That all changed on the evening of March 9, 1944. Estonians remember the horrors of that night much in the same way Americans remember September 11, 2001. That is the night when the Soviet air force launched a massive air attack on Tallinn.

We had just finished our supper when, without any warning from air-raid sirens, I heard the clacking sound of anti-aircraft fire. It was more intense than usual. I opened the front door and noticed the orange-colored sky over Tallinn, brightly illuminated by countless flares that slowly descended upon the city. I had seen these parachute-suspended flares, nicknamed "Stalin's Christmas trees," during previous air raids and knew that deadly bombs were about to follow. Moments later, I heard the first explosions. No need to be alarmed, I thought. It's just another bomb attack on the harbor or railroad yards.

As the thunder of the explosions grew louder, I sensed that this attack was different from any previous ones. Uncle Haakon suggested that we should seek cover. We considered going to the dugout shelter in the yard, but decided against it because of the freezing weather. We ruled out the basement for the same reason. The next safest place was the windowless bathroom in the middle of the house. We knew it would offer protection from shrapnel and broken glass, although not from a direct bomb hit. We grabbed several blankets and pillows and rushed into the bathroom. There were seven of us huddled quietly in that small space: Aunt Senta, Uncle Haakon, their children Andres and Marike, Grandmother, my mother, and I. Our dog Miku, who usually liked to show off his bravery, crawled under my legs and looked just as frightened as we were. Marike, who had just celebrated her third birthday four days earlier, sat quietly on her mother's lap, seemingly unaware of the danger.

After another round of bombs we lost electric power, which threw us into total darkness until we could find a flashlight and light a candle. We sat in silence, paying attention only to the sound of the bomb explosions. Each time we heard the whistling of falling bombs, we crouched and hoped that our lives would be spared. Another loud explosion caused the walls to shake. Marike started to cry. The air became stifling. As soon as there was a break in the barrage, we opened the door for fresh air, but had to close it as soon as the pounding started again.

Finally, after more than two hours, everything quieted down and we dared to go outside and look around. The sky above the city was embraced in an eerie orange glow, and the air was filled with the bitter smell of smoke. A quick inspection of the house revealed that only one window was broken in the living room. Tired and shaken by the terrifying experience, we went to bed, but our sleep was unexpectedly disrupted by a second wave of bombings at around one in the morning. We rushed back to the bathroom, clad in pajamas and robes. This time the explosions seemed more distant, giving us hope that our neighborhood would be spared. The pummeling went on for another two hours until it finally died down, and we were able to go back to bed.

A gray cloud of smoke and ashes greeted us the next morning when we tried to assess what had happened the previous night. We could not grasp the full extent of the damages, but it was clear from the smoke that the city had suffered severe fire damage from incendiary bombs. The damage was unlike that of any of the previous air raids, which had been directed at specific military targets. My mother and Uncle Haakon decided to go to the city, hoping that the pharmacy and his office would still be there. Because trains and buses were not running, they had to walk more than four miles to reach the city center, with Miku loyally following them.

I ventured out, looking for signs of devastation in the area. One home on our street appeared to be seriously damaged, and the bombs had left a couple of gaping craters a few streets further away. I heard that the schools were closed, so I stayed home for the rest of the day and waited for my mother to come home. She arrived in the late afternoon, her hat and clothing covered with soot and ashes from the smoldering fires.

"Thank God, the pharmacy survived," she reported with a sigh of relief. "A nearby building, close to city hall, was hit by a bomb, and the buildings on Harju Street are totally demolished. There is nothing left of your father's favorite restaurant, Kuld Lõvi (The Golden Lion)." She wiped soot off her forehead, and added, "The Estonia Theater was hit by an incendiary bomb and caught fire. There was a ballet performance going on when the attack began, but I heard that most people were able to escape. The dancers escaped too, dashing through the streets in their fancy tights and tutus."

Uncle Haakon returned hours later and confirmed that the air raid had inflicted widespread damage throughout the city. Neighborhoods with older wooden houses had been engulfed by huge firestorms and many buildings were still smoldering. Late in the evening, Miku appeared at the kitchen doorstep, tired and thirsty. He looked more like a wild animal than the well-groomed white spitz that had left the house in the morning; his natural white fur had turned to a dark charcoal from snooping through the ruins. It took more than one bath to restore the shine to his thick white fur.

This dreadful experience left my whole family in shock. In one night, everything had suddenly changed. The day before the attack, we had celebrated Aunt Senta's birthday. The day after, we could only celebrate being alive and having a roof over our heads.

The clubhouse, my temporary school building, had suffered only minor damages. Yet, it was deemed unsafe and all classes were cancelled indefinitely. I was happy to hear the news. Though I loved school, I hated the long trek and the incredibly crowded, poorly heated classroom.

According to the official report, 757 people were killed in that one night, and 659 were injured. 1,549 buildings were destroyed, leaving more than 20,000 people in Tallinn without shelter. It was the most devastating attack on an Estonian city during the whole war.

The massive bombing attack left everyone in the country distraught and edgy. Would there be other air attacks? Where would we be safe? These concerns were on everyone's minds and filled our daily conversations. Another attack nearly demolished the northeastern coastal city of Narva, and the university town of Tartu suffered major damage from multiple bombing raids.

Uncle Haakon's office was evacuated to Rapla, a small town about thirty miles south of Tallinn. He went there without delay, and Aunt Senta, Grandmother, and the children joined him shortly thereafter. My mother had to remain at her job at the pharmacy. Uncle Karli invited me to his farm, where I had spent the past two summers, but my mother thought it was too close to the front; it wasn't prudent to be separated in those unsettled times. Besides, I was about to graduate from the elementary school and had to be ready to return in case school reopened. So I stayed in our home in Nõmme.

The school never opened, but since the school year was almost over, all students in my class were issued graduation diplomas. I received a letter inviting me to Hiiu Gymnasium on May 6, 1944—my thirteenth birthday—to receive my diploma. I couldn't think of a better birthday gift.

When I awoke that morning, an overnight snowfall had blanketed the whole neighborhood with a thick layer of fresh snow. This was a real surprise because snow in May was highly unusual, even in a Nordic country like Estonia. It was perfect day to use Cousin Eda's Finnish sled, also known as a kick sled. It was very popular both in Finland and Estonia in those days. It consisted of a chair mounted on a pair of metal runners. The handlebars on top of its back provided the means for steering. Instead of taking the local bus, I hopped on the sled and kicked my way to Hiiu Gymnasium. It was pure joy to stand on a runner and pick up speed by kicking the ground with the other foot. I had never imagined doing that on my birthday.

To my surprise and disappointment, there was no graduation ceremony. I received only a few congratulatory words from a teacher who handed me my diploma, which entitled me to enroll in a Gymnasium in the fall. By that time, however, conditions on the war front had worsened to the point that all my plans for further schooling were shattered.

Although the men of the Estonian Legion were able to stop the Russian Army, we were still deeply concerned about our safety. How long would the Germany Army—fighting on two fronts after the Allied invasion in Normandy—be able to hold the Eastern front? I remember buying a daily newspaper every morning at the newsstand across from the train station and devouring every bit of news from the front on my walk home. I was proud to read about four Estonian fighters who had had been awarded the Knights Cross of the Iron Cross, the highest German military award for bravery. One afternoon, at the Nõmme train station, I got the thrill of actually seeing one of these heroes, Sergeant Harald Nugiseks. He was not more than a few yards away from me, the Knight's Cross in plain view on the front of his collar. I just stood there and gazed at him with awe until he turned and disappeared into the crowd.

With a new offensive in July, the Red Army succeeded in occupying the city of Narva in the north and crossed the Estonian border in the south. Many Estonians started to plan for the ominous eventuality they had feared all along—fleeing the homeland and leaving their homes with all their belongings behind. For my family, life under another Soviet occupation was not an option; the previous reign of terror was still fresh in our minds.

We had only two choices: we could go to either Sweden or Germany, but each option involved certain risks. Clearly, Sweden was our preferred destination. As a peaceful country, it would provide welcome relief from the terrors and sufferings of the war. However, it was impossible to legally go to Sweden. It had to be done secretly under the cover of darkness in private motorboats, evading German border-patrol boats, while hoping to survive the treacherous waters of the Baltic Sea. Furthermore, many people couldn't afford the sky-high prices demanded by the boat operators.

The second option—sailing to Germany—had been always available. It was even encouraged by the authorities because the German war industry was in a dire need of labor. But working in a Nazi munitions factory under the repeated bombardment of Allied air raids did not appeal to most Estonians. Sailing itself was also treacherous; there was the chance of being torpedoed at sea by Soviet bombers. So we waited like the bird during a forest fire that sits in her nest and doesn't fly off until the flames arrive.

The flames of war were approaching rapidly and they would soon engulf our nests. By the end of August, the Soviets had taken the city of Tartu and the news from the front became more disheartening with each day. As the war in Finland was winding down, our Finnish Boys returned to Estonia after receiving amnesty from the Germans, in order to take part in the defense against the Red Army. But that was not enough to contain the onslaught from the East. As the German Army planned for a retreat from Estonia, we came to the somber realization that it was high time to start planning for our departure as well.

Grandmother and Aunt Senta with her children returned from the country, with Uncle Haakon to follow later. It was a tremendous relief to see them. With most of our family together, we could finally make preparations for our departure.

We collected our most important personal documents and small valuables in one place. My most precious possession was my stamp collection. I had accumulated a sizable assortment of stamps, organized neatly by countries in a large album. Since it was too bulky to take it with me, I selected a set of the most valuable stamps, dropped it into a cellophane envelope, and placed it next to our important documents.

My mother laid our silver dinnerware and crystal on the dinner table so that she could decide what to take with us. She selected several small silver spoons and knives because they could be readily traded for food or transportation. Larger items were to remain behind, hidden in a safe place. I dug a hole in the backyard where we buried them, neatly packed in a metal box in which Aunt Elli, who was an avid painter, used to store her paints. After filling the hole with sand, I covered it carefully with moss, and measured and recorded its coordinates so that the treasures could be found and recovered at a later time.

Not knowing how we would leave, we divided everything into categories of importance: absolutely essential items were at the top of the list; followed by the next important; with nice-to-have things at the bottom. The overriding consideration was that we should be able to carry them without any help. That meant one suitcase in each hand

and a rucksack on the back. We burned all documents, newspapers, magazines, and books that could raise the ire of communist occupiers because we did not want to endanger the lives of the people who might wind up living in the house. Then we started to pack while we waited for Uncle Haakon to come and help us make the most important decisions of our lives—how and when to make our getaway.

10

The Last Train

UNCLE HAAKON WAS the rock of our family. He gave us the strength and stability that we badly needed in those unsettling days. Smart and levelheaded, he got things done quietly, without much fanfare. I couldn't think of anyone more dependable and better informed than Uncle Haakon. Fluent in German and English, he managed to deal effectively with the occupying Nazi administration during the day, while listening secretly to BBC News at night. He had reached the conclusion that it was only a matter of time before Germany would lose the war. Meanwhile, he knew that it was of utmost importance to save our family from again falling under Soviet occupation. We urgently needed his presence and great acumen to assess the rapidly changing situation and plan for our escape.

But Uncle Haakon was thirty miles away in his office, and his strong sense of duty would keep him there until he had completed his work and left instructions to others to take over. Only then would he be able to come home to us. He traveled by bicycle, because the bus and train services had become erratic and were no longer dependable. First, he went directly to Tallinn to deliver some office documents, and then he tried to make travel arrangements for all of us.

When Uncle Haakon finally arrived home in the late afternoon, he looked tired and despondent. "Most of the German-bound ships have already left," he said. "Only two ships are still in the harbor. One is a passenger ship; the other is a military-hospital ship, which also has many Estonians on board. Both are overcrowded and should be leaving any moment. But there are still many people waiting in the harbor, hoping to get on board at the last minute." He paused, took a couple of puffs on his pipe, and said with a sigh, "The German Army is leaving, and the Russian tanks could be here any time." An aura of gloom descended upon us like a dark cloud. I felt as if the oxygen had left the room. We had missed our last chance to escape to Germany! We sat in stunned silence, feeling trapped and scared.

The only option left for us was to flee by land to the west coast, where we might find someone with a motorboat to take us to Sweden. Uncle Haakon had heard from a friend that a special train for railroad employees was leaving from Nõmme for the coastal city of Haapsalu the next morning. "We should try to catch that train," he said. "I can pretend to be someone from the railroad office, if necessary."

Suddenly, our discussion was interrupted by an unexpected phone call. It was from Uncle Artur's brother, Leo Puksov. I remembered him as a tall, unpretentious man with a pleasant smile. Having fled from the fighting on the southern front in a horse-drawn wagon, he was on his way to see us. He was concerned about our safety and wanted to help us with transportation, in case we needed it. That was truly a godsend—he came just when we needed him most.

Leo arrived in about an hour. "I'm glad I was able to find you," he said as he jumped off his wagon. "I knew it would be dangerous for you to stay and thought I might be able to help. I even brought my rifle to protect us from any trouble," he added, pointing to where the weapon was hidden in the wagon. As the chief forester, he had a permit to carry it.

As Uncle Haakon and Leo made plans, we heard a series of explosions coming from the direction of the city. "This is it," said Uncle Haakon. "The Germans are now blowing up whatever they can. That means that they'll be gone by tomorrow. We have to get out of here as soon as possible. We must catch that special train first thing in the morning. If we can't, I hope Leo's horse can outrun the Soviet tanks."

Uncle Haakon left the room and returned with a bottle of vodka and two shot glasses.

"Oh, these men," my mother grumbled. "At a time like this, exactly when they need a clear mind, they have to drink." In her opinion even a single alcoholic drink was one too many.

The men ignored her comments and proceeded to commemorate their decision with a couple of shots. Then they decided to finish packing and get a few winks of sleep. I, too, tried to get some sleep, but the events of the day and the rumble of the explosions kept me up through most of the night.

The next morning, we arose before dawn. It was Friday, September 22, 1944. The sky was clear, and streaks of early morning sunlight were shining through the pine trees. As we made final preparations for leaving, Grandmother expressed some doubts. "I am an old woman, and I don't think the communists will hurt me," she said. "I am worried about Karli. I don't know what is happening to him. If he hasn't left his farm, then I want to stay."

My mother told her that he probably had escaped already, and if not, he would be either arrested or deported to Siberia because of the strong anti-communist statements he had made in public. "So you'd better come with us, otherwise you'll regret it," she insisted.

"I think you are right. I just hope that he managed to get out in time," Grandmother sighed and continued packing. Aunt Iti, who had joined us a few days earlier, also had misgivings, but finally agreed to come along.

My mother gave me Eda's ski suit to wear because it was ideal for travel, and would be suitable for everyday wear later. She made me put on two sets of underwear in order to have more space in the suitcase. She also packed a few bottles of alcohol in case we needed to buy transportation or passage through checkpoints. We loaded our baggage onto Leo's wagon, left the house keys with Aunt Elli's former maid Miili, and started to head toward the Nõmme train station. Grandmother and Marike sat on the wagon, while the rest of us followed on foot, with Miku faithfully behind us.

When we came within sight of the station, we noticed a long train of passenger cars parked on a track that was normally used for freight trains. With raised hopes and quickened pace, we moved forward.

"Is this train going to Haapsalu?" Uncle Haakon asked an elderly man who was leaning out of a window.

"I hope so," he replied. "But we don't know for sure. We don't even have an engine yet." Noticing our baggage, he warned, "The train is already full."

Unwilling to accept the man's answer, we started to check the cars on our own. Going from one car to the next, we learned that he was right—all compartments were jam-packed with people and their belongings of all shapes and sizes. Our hopes were fading fast.

As we reached the last car at the end of the train, Uncle Haakon discovered a couple of unoccupied seats. "Go in fast," he whispered. "Don't ask any questions. Just squeeze in before anyone can challenge us." Grandmother and the children went in first, followed by the baggage and the rest of our group. We didn't care that we were wedged on top of our suitcases—we felt lucky to be on board. All we needed now was an engine.

We learned from fellow passengers that the train was, indeed, reserved for the railroad workers, and it had been scheduled to leave earlier in the morning. It was already mid-afternoon and everyone was becoming increasingly concerned about the delay. Why hadn't the engine come? When would it come? Or would it come at all? These frightening questions were on everyone's mind.

Suddenly, Aunt Iti peeked into her purse. She looked worried. "I don't have many cigarettes left," she gasped. "I have to go and get more from my friend who works for the cigarette company. She lives not far from here. I'll be back soon." Despite my mother's warnings that she might miss the train, she grabbed her carrying bag, stepped off the train, and left.

A while later, a man from the street walked up to the train and announced, "The Russians are already in Tallinn. The tanks are on Vabaduse Väljak." A murmur of alarm went through the train. "My

God!" someone howled. "They are only six kilometers away from us. We need to get going. Where is the engine they promised?"

Everyone sat in silence, fretting and praying for that engine to arrive. The unbearable tension was finally broken by a loud jolt. It came from the coupling of the long-awaited engine to the train, raising our hopes for an imminent departure.

While everyone seemed relieved, my mother was in a panic. "Where is Aunt Iti?" she shrieked. Aunt Iti was still missing. I remember an awfully helpless feeling, realizing there was nothing we could do for her. I looked out of the window and saw Uncle Haakon step off the train to look for her. He returned empty-handed. And still there was no sight of Aunt Iti. Only Miku was still sitting there, his sad gaze longingly following my every move. Leaving him behind was painful, but knowing that that Miili would take care of him gave me some comfort. She had done it before when Aunt Elli's family was deported and she would do the same now.

Finally, the doors closed and the train began to move. Aunt Iti had missed the last train! It was a high price to pay for a few packs of cigarettes.

Only years later, did I hear from my mother that cigarettes had been only a pretext for missing the train. The real reason was that Aunt Iti wanted to remain close to her secret boyfriend in Tallinn.

Gathering speed, the train passed through familiar neighborhoods and the local stations of Hiiu, Kivimäe, and Pääsküla. Before long, we were rolling past weatherbeaten farmhouses in the midst of recently harvested wheat and rye fields. I breathed an enormous sigh of relief—thank God, we were getting out. I shuddered at the thought that we could have been left behind, as Aunt Iti was, had we not been able to get to the train on time. What would happen to her? And what about my friends and classmates? Had they been able to escape? And what would happen to us next? We had been lucky so far, but I wondered if we would we be lucky enough to find a passage to Sweden before the Soviet tanks reached the coast of Haapsalu.

Eventually, the monotonous rhythm of the train made me drowsy and I fell asleep. I don't recall how long I slept before I was awakened by a jolt. The train was no longer moving. In the predawn darkness, I saw that we had stopped in the middle of a forest. Why wasn't the train moving? Had the German Army blocked it, or had we run out of fuel? Everyone waited warily for some explanation. "Maybe the conductor is a communist and wants us to be captured by the Russians," a frightened passenger speculated, adding more fuel to the tension.

Uncle Haakon and another man went to investigate, leaving us anxiously waiting. He returned shortly to calm the crowd. "There is nothing to worry about," he said. "We are already near Haapsalu. The Russians bombed it last night, and the conductor is afraid that the tracks may have been damaged. He is waiting until daylight before he can go on safely." I could almost hear the sigh of relief in the silent darkness.

Shortly after sunrise, the train started to move. It slowed to a crawl when we reached the outskirts of Haapsalu. Finally, we arrived at the train station there. I was surprised to find it eerily deserted. We stepped down to the empty platform. There was only an abandoned baggage cart with a couple of cases of soft drinks. Several of us grabbed a bottle or two to quench our thirst and refresh our dehydrated bodies. But apparently the bottles had been in the hot sun too long and the warm, sweet, lemon-flavored soda was anything but refreshing. Nor was that sticky liquid good for washing and cleaning up, as some of us found out the hard way.

Our goal was to reach Rohuküla Harbor, about seven miles west of the city, but there were neither buses nor taxis in sight. Eventually, a fellow passenger from our train, Robert Teene, managed to find a farmer with a horse-drawn wagon.

When the farmer heard that we needed transportation to the harbor, he shook his head in disbelief. "Are you crazy? It's dangerous to go there. The Russians are bombing the harbor. Can't you see?" He pointed toward the billowing smoke in the distance. No amount of money could change his mind. "The German marks will be worthless under the Russians," he said.

Luckily, my mother remembered the alcohol bottles in her suit-case. "We can pay with alcohol," she said. The sight of the bottle had a miraculous effect on the farmer. All of a sudden, he lost all fear and declared, "The bombing will be over by the time we get there. So let's go."

Together with Robert Teene, his wife, and daughter Maie, we loaded our suitcases on top of his wagon and started our journey to the harbor. We followed the same routine as in Nõmme, with Grand-mother and Marike on the wagon, and the rest of us slogging behind on foot.

Shortly after we left the city, we were attacked by a low-flying airplane. "Hit the ground. Everybody into the ditch," someone yelled. I jumped into the roadside ditch, stayed in a prone position, and held my breath. "Rat-a-tat-a-ta-a ..." came the machine-gun fire from the Soviet fighter plane, strafing the road, forming dust clouds where the bullets hit the ground. A second plane followed, spraying us with an-other shower of bullets before disappearing into the sky. Terrified, we remained frozen in the ditch until we felt safe enough to get up. Fortunately, we all escaped unscathed. Shaken by the experience, we brushed our clothes and continued walking, wary of new attacks.

The farmer decided to calm his shattered nerves by mixing himself a stiff drink from the alcohol we had given him earlier. It seemed that he needed several drinks to recover from the harrowing experience. By the time we reached the harbor, he was totally inebriated.

The entire harbor area swarmed with retreating German soldiers and horses. The smell of horses was everywhere. I was astonished that horses were still used so widely in modern warfare.

As soon as the farmer saw the horses, his eyes lit up and he beamed. "These Germans," he said, "they won't need these horses anymore, but I do." He unharnessed his jade and hurriedly exchanged it for a young, spirited black horse. After the horse was harnessed, he jumped on the wagon, waved us good-bye, and trotted away.

Except for the German soldiers and their horses, the harbor was almost deserted. There were no private boats to be found. We heard that anyone who owned a motorboat had left for Sweden days earlier. The news shattered our hopes of finding a passage to Sweden.

A German officer who appeared to be in charge told Uncle Haakon that he was evacuating his troops to Heltermaa on the coast of Hiiumaa, the second largest island off the Estonian mainland. Then they would be ferried over to Saaremaa, the largest island with a major commercial port. From there, they would go by military transport ships to Germany. He thought those ships would evacuate civilian refugees as well.

"Today," the officer said, "the ferries are busy moving my company. But tomorrow, they can evacuate you, too. Meanwhile, you might find overnight shelter in the empty warehouse." He pointed to a large nondescript gray building near the pier.

When he heard that we were hungry and thirsty, he ordered one of his soldiers to bring us bread and water. This was the first time I had tasted German Army bread. It was in the shape of an oversized brown brick, dry and hard, as if it had been lying around for several days. But it didn't matter—any food would have satisfied our hungry stomachs.

It was getting dark when we arrived at the abandoned warehouse. As we stepped inside the musty building, we found ourselves in total darkness. Stumbling like blind men, we tried to find our way until we settled down at a spot along a wall. As we piled our belongings and prepared makeshift bedding on the dirt floor, my fingers touched something soft and sticky. I couldn't see what it was, but the obnoxious smell left no doubt in my mind.

"I think I have some dog poop here," I whispered to my mother. "Do you have anything for cleaning my fingers?"

"Oh my God! Oh no," she moaned. That really must have upset her because she was always finicky about cleanliness and personal hygiene. She lit a match to determine the extent of the damage. "You have it all over your fingers and your coat, too," she grumbled as she opened a bottle of alcohol for cleaning and disinfecting. That was the second time on our journey when alcohol saved our day.

We moved to another area and examined it carefully before settling down. In the darkness I heard my mother cry. The day's events had put just too much strain on her. Trying to deal with everything we had just been through was strenuous for me as well. Twisting and turning, I was unable to get much sleep on the cold, lumpy ground.

The next morning, we collected our belongings and rushed back to the pier. The officer in charge had kept his word. "Get ready to board the next ferry as soon as it arrives," he shouted. The moment it arrived, we wasted no time in getting on board. The ferry rapidly filled way beyond its capacity. There was a mix of German soldiers and Estonian families on the run from the Soviet menace. The soldiers looked tired in their untidy uniforms; they no longer resembled the victorious troops who had liberated us from the Soviet terror three years earlier. Looking at these dejected men, Uncle Haakon remarked, "This is an army in retreat. If we had to depend on these soldiers to keep the Russians out, we'd never have gotten away. Only the men of the Estonian Legion kept the Russians at bay long enough for us to escape."

As the ferry pulled away, I saw the look of relief on people's faces. They knew—we all did—that we would be out of immediate danger as soon as we arrived on Hiiumaa. A twelve-mile-wide bay would then separate us from the mainland and put us out of reach of Soviet tanks. And maybe, if we were lucky, we might find someone on the island to take us to Sweden. We held on to that glimmer of hope.

11

Fleeing from Island to Island

A T HELTERMAA HARBOR we were met by an officer who appeared to be in charge of coordinating both military and civilian evacuations. He told us to go to Orjaku, where we would be able to catch a ferry to Saaremaa. None of us had heard of Orjaku or knew how far it was from Heltermaa. Noticing our bewilderment, the officer explained, "It's twenty-five kilometers south. We have trucks to take you there."

We boarded one of the waiting army trucks while our baggage was loaded on another, and soon our convoy was off to Orjaku. We rumbled along a dusty country road for a while until we were suddenly stopped at a checkpoint. A soldier came and lowered the tailgate. "The Wehrmacht needs the truck," he said. "You have to get off now."

"But our baggage is on the other truck," Uncle Haakon protested.

"That truck can go on to Orjaku, but you have to get off and walk. It's less than ten kilometers from here." When he noticed the children, he allowed Grandmother, Aunt Senta, and the children to get on the baggage truck.

"Don't worry, I'll keep an eye on our luggage," shouted Aunt Senta in her typical spunky fashion. "I'll see you in Orjaku."

We gathered everyone who was left on the road and started to walk. At first, it felt good to stretch our legs and breathe fresh air after the bumpy ride in a dusty truck.

Hiiumaa countryside, dotted with countless juniper bushes, was similar to that of the neighboring Vormsi Island. It reminded me of my marvelous summer there, my last vacation before the war, when Father was still with us. At that time, no one could have imagined that we'd be here five years later, running from the Russian Army.

Eventually, the long trek started to take its toll on us. We had to stop to rest and wonder how much farther we would have to drag ourselves on the windy dirt road. We were greatly relieved when the houses of Orjaku came within sight. Finally, we'd be able to reunite with our loved ones and our belongings. But then we met a man who told us that the women and children with our baggage never went to Orjaku; they had been left on a roadside near another village.

As we changed course and headed towards that village, my mother muttered, "I hope he knows what he's talking about."

Fortunately, the man did know. Our long slog finally ended when we found the women and children sitting on our suitcases along the roadside exactly where the man had told us they would be. Words cannot describe our relief at seeing them there, not to mention the baggage, which contained the only possessions we still had. There were moments when I had had serious doubts if I would ever again see my suitcase and my precious stamp collection.

"Thank God, you are here," yelled Aunt Senta. "I was afraid you'd never find us. They dumped us here because we didn't have permits to get into the harbor."

"Damn the Germans," Uncle Haakon griped. "They need a permit for everything. Now I must go and find where to get them." He took off with Mr. Teene, leaving the rest of us waiting on the chilly roadside. They seemed to be gone forever, but when they finally did return, I could tell from their beaming faces that they had been successful. "At last, we got them," said Uncle Haakon. "Permits for everyone on the ferry tomorrow morning. All we need now is a place to spend the night."

We were fortunate to find a local farmer who was willing to feed us and provide overnight shelter in his barn. Although his living from his small farm was no doubt modest, he and his wife went out of their way to make us welcome. At last, we were able wash ourselves with clean water and have our first hot meal since leaving home. The dinner table included delicacies we hadn't seen for a long time: delicious sausages and bacon with sauerkraut, potatoes with mushroom sauce, all accompanied by rye bread and butter. We devoured everything as if it was our last meal.

After the dinner, the farmer shared some schnapps with Uncle Haakon. He confirmed our fears that anyone with a seaworthy motorboat had already left for either Sweden or Finland. "And the fishermen who are staying," he added, "have hidden their boats, afraid that some desperate men might take them at gunpoint and rob them of their livelihood. Besides, I wouldn't recommend crossing the Baltic Sea in a small fishing boat. I've heard that too many people have lost their lives attempting to do that. Your best bet is to go to Saaremaa tomorrow morning and get on board of one of the military ships leaving for Germany."

Those words left no doubt in our minds that we needed to abandon our dream of going to Sweden, and strive to reach Germany before it was too late even to do that. With these troubled thoughts, we separated for the night.

As I was climbing the ladder to the hayloft in the barn to rest my tired bones, the ascent seemed like going to heaven. The intoxicating scent of hay brought back sweet memories of my summers on Uncle Karli's farm. And when I sank into the soft cushion of hay, it felt as though all my worries were swept away. I fell asleep, happy and contented.

The next morning, a horse-drawn wagon that Mr. Teene had arranged for us the night before was waiting to take our luggage to Orjaku Harbor. It was the same routine as on the way to Rohuküla, with Grandmother and the children sitting on the wagon and the rest of us following on foot.

When we reached the small harbor, it was already crowded with people and their belongings. Everyone hoped to find transportation to the big island. An army officer instructed us to join the crowd and wait for the next ferry.

While we were waiting, Uncle Haakon heard a German officer mention that Haapsalu had fallen to the Russians the day before. We had been lucky to be on one of the very last ferries leaving the mainland before the Soviet tanks reached Rohuküla Harbor.

When the ferry arrived, we discovered that it was an open raft floating on pontoons, much smaller than the one we had taken the day before. I heard someone question its ability to get us safely across the choppy sea. However, the soldiers operating the rafts seemed to know what they were doing as they helped us to board the wobbly structure. Despite the rough waters, we managed to make the crossing without any mishaps.

We came ashore in Triigi Harbor, where a crew of military personnel helped us off the raft and gave us bread and water. Then they put us on trucks heading directly to Kuressaare, where ships would be ready to evacuate us. Our canvas-covered vehicle was filled to capacity, with our baggage piled in the middle and the rest of us squeezed onto two benches on each side. On top of the luggage sat Uncle Haakon's water-soaked Borsalino hat, which the wind had blown into the water when he stepped off the raft.

Soon after we left, it started to rain. We stopped and the driver closed the rear curtain. It did keep the rain out, but it also cut us off from fresh air. After a while, the stifling air, mixed with exhaust fumes, became too much for the girl sitting next to me. Suddenly, she turned to me and said, "I am getting sick." Then she proceeded to throw up, spilling some of her vomit onto my shoes and pants. Thanks to my mother's help, I was able to clean up most of the damage, but the horrible stench lingered. But who cared—we were about to reach the ship that would take us away from it all.

Unfortunately, that ship turned out to be an elusive dream. As we reached the outskirts of Kuressaare, the truck came to an unexpected stop. An army officer appeared and announced, "You can't go any farther. The city is flooded with refugees and is off limits to new arrivals. There are absolutely no accommodations within the city. You have to turn around and go to Kallemäe. You can stay there in the local schoolhouse and wait for the next ship."

"When will that happen?" several people shouted almost in unison.

"I don't know. Perhaps in a couple of days," replied the officer.

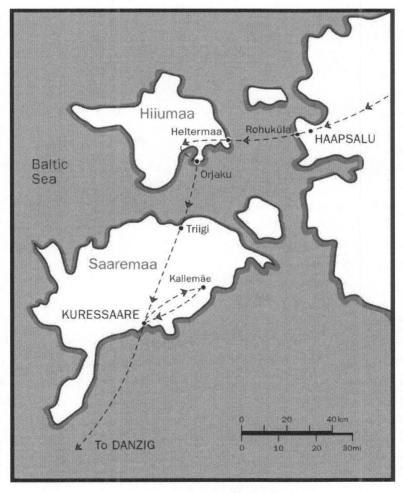

Our escape trail through the islands

Our hope to reach the ship before the end of the day had been dealt a crushing blow. The driver started the engine and we were on our way to a place that no one knew.

The trip to Kallemäe seemed to go on forever. Finally, we stopped in front of an impressive two-story schoolhouse that would be our temporary shelter. The inside of the building bore no resemblance to a school. Instead of rows of classroom seats, there were bunk beds, empty boxes, and a few discarded army uniforms scattered around the rooms. The caretaker told us that the building had been used by the Wehrmacht as a hospital and a quartermaster center.

We discovered that there were not enough bunks for everyone, so some of us had to double up or sleep on the floor. I shared a top bunk with Maie. Both of us were ill at ease, and embarrassed by the arrangement, but it was better than sleeping on the floor. We were at that awkward age, not knowing whether to treat the other as a child or a young adult.

The following day was filled with anxiety and nervous waiting. Tensions nearly reached a breaking point when we heard that the Soviet Army had taken total control of the mainland. Now it was only a matter of days before the army would land on Saaremaa, most likely on an area about twenty miles east from us.

We took endless walks around the schoolhouse to pass the time and calm our nerves. We couldn't wander very far because we had to be ready to leave at a moment's notice. Our favorite pastime was picking hazelnuts from the trees in the schoolyard. The nuts added tasty nourishment to the food we bought from the local store, and the challenge of crunching them without nutcrackers kept us busy.

After languishing in Kallemäe for two days and nights, the long-awaited moment of departure finally arrived. We were overjoyed when a small convoy of military trucks came to our rescue and took us to Kuressaare. When we reached the city, I noticed two ships anchored in the harbor. I could feel my heart beating faster—escape was finally within our reach.

As we joined the crowd on the market square, Grandmother spotted a family friend who brought welcome news about Uncle Karli. "I saw him and his wife here yesterday," he said. "They are well and should be on the big ship by now."

Grandmother, who had been agonizing about his fate throughout the journey, brightened visibly as tears of happiness streamed down her cheeks. "Thank God, he is safe," she said. "Now my mind is at ease. Hopefully, I'll see him soon."

As I kept a longing watch on the ships, I noticed a cloud of black smoke billowing from the big ship. "Look," a woman screamed, "the ship is on fire." An officer came and confirmed that the ship had, indeed, caught fire. "It's under control," he said to calm us. "But the captain is not accepting any more refugees today. Come back tomorrow morning."

Our hopes were crushed again and replaced with new worries and fears. Could the ships still accommodate us? How safe are the ships? Would the Soviet bombers attack us? Where could we find shelter for the night? All these thoughts raced through our minds as we contemplated our next move.

Someone in our group knew the director of the local veterinary clinic and called him for advice. He said that since the clinic was closed, we could spend the night there. When he unlocked the doors for us, we were greeted with a peculiar odor reminiscent of its former residents. But that didn't bother us as long as there was adequate space to sleep on the floor.

As we were about to settle in for the night, I heard a loud commotion outside. Suddenly, the door swung open and a dark-haired, unshaven man barged in brandishing a gun that looked exactly like the Nagant revolver I had found in the forest after the Soviet retreat. His menacing eyes swept around the room.

"Here you are, you damned Nazi lovers," he snarled. "You thought you were going to get away, ah? But you aren't going anywhere because I'm going to kill you! All of you!"

He pointed the weapon at us in a slow sweeping motion. He smelled as if he had been drinking heavily, apparently celebrating the anticipated arrival of his communist comrades. His bloodshot eyes, filled with anger, revealed the seriousness of his deadly intentions.

Petrified, everyone froze in place. I lowered my body slowly to the floor and waited. Is he really going to shoot? I wondered. Maybe he was just threatening.

Uncle Haakon, who happened to be near the gunman, cautiously approached him and said, "I am sorry, but you must be mistaken. We're not Nazi supporters. We are just innocent families with children and old people." I don't recall what else he said, but somehow he managed to pacify the gunman and escort him out of the building. We barricaded the door with furniture to keep him from returning, and the men kept vigil throughout the night.

Only after I had recovered from the shock of this terrifying ordeal did I grasp the seriousness of what had happened. That was a close call—we really could have been killed or wounded. How ironic, to have survived Soviet bombs and bullets only to be gunned down by a communist thug just hours before getting away. These thoughts, and the anticipation of the long-awaited journey, kept me awake throughout the night.

We left the clinic at daybreak in order to be the first in line for the next available ship. But when we arrived at the town square, it was already bustling with people. The commanding officer assured us that we would be able to board as soon as the trucks arrived to take us to Roomassaare Harbor, four kilometers down the road.

As we approached the harbor, I noticed that the big ship was still smoking, a sign that the fire hadn't been completely extinguished. Is the ship still seaworthy? I wondered. Could the fire break out later and cause an inferno at sea? All these possibilities flashed through my mind. Only when I noticed that the tenders were heading toward the smaller ship, was I able to calm down. Thank God, we will not go on that burning ship!

The boarding process was slow and complicated. It felt almost too long to the impatient crowd on shore. First, we had to board a tender, which was a small, wobbly raft floating on pontoons. We held on to each other for balance as the tender swayed through the waves and salty mist toward the ship. Then we had to climb like monkeys, one by one, on rope ladders to reach the ship's deck. Some of us struggled, especially the women and old people. But no one complained—these were the final steps of our getaway.

Our ship was a small military cargo ship, *Füsiler II*, with three large cargo compartments. Our group was ushered into the middle one through a wide hatchway door. We found ourselves together with about two hundred people, crowded into one musty cargo compartment. After we retrieved our luggage, which had been hoisted on board by a shipboard winch, there was barely enough room for us to lie on the floor.

This was my first time on a big ship, and naturally, I had to explore it to satisfy my curiosity. I saw several anti-aircraft guns on the main deck. Their barrels, pointing toward the sky, kept reminding me of the of the ever-present Soviet bomber threat.

As I wandered toward the forward section, I noticed a couple of armed German soldiers guarding the entryway to the forward cargo room. Suddenly, a disheveled man with a bucket in hand appeared from the hatchway door. He was wearing a shabby Russian Army uniform—the marks of stripped-off military insignia were clearly visible. The guards allowed him to go to the railing, where he dumped the contents overboard. Seconds later, an awful stench reached my nostrils, leaving no doubt what had been in the bucket.

I didn't understand what was going on until a man standing next to me explained. "The forward and aft cargo rooms are full of Russian prisoners of war. I heard that there are almost five thousand of them. They all are packed into the same size cargo rooms as ours. They must be standing like sardines in a tin can, with no room for movement. The bucket the man is carrying must be full of their bodily fluids. ..." I didn't hear the rest of his explanation because I had to rush away for fresh air.

It puzzled me why the Germans would bother bringing Russian prisoners to Germany. When I got back to our compartment, I told Uncle Haakon about it and asked, "Why would they do it?"

"They'll become forced laborers in the German war industry," he explained. "With all able-bodied men fighting on two fronts, Germany is short of workers."

Toward late afternoon, the large smoldering ship left the port, escorted by a small naval vessel. We waved at the departing passengers, hoping that our ship would follow them soon. But to our dismay, more prisoners were brought on board, and our departure was delayed until late next afternoon.

As our ship finally started to move, everyone in our cargo compartment rushed to the deck to get a last glimpse of the homeland. I saw many people in tears—tears of sadness as well as tears of joy—as we waved good-bye to the disappearing coastline.

"This is probably the last time I will see my homeland," Grandmother wailed. She and many people of her generation appeared heartbroken to leave their friends and lifelong accomplishments behind. For many others, including me, it was also a moment of sadness, but mainly one of relief and liberation.

Soon we were on the open sea, leaving the fear of being caught by the Soviet occupation forces behind us. But now we faced a new danger—the threat of Soviet air attacks. My biggest fear was that our ship would be sunk by an air-launched torpedo and I would drown in the cold waters of the Baltic Sea. While waiting in Kuressaare, we had received the shocking news that two ships that left Tallinn had become victims of such an attack.

One of the ships, *Moero*, which was carrying wounded soldiers and Estonian civilians, had been torpedoed and sunk even though it was clearly marked as a hospital ship. Most of its passengers perished in the Baltic Sea. The other ship, *RO-22*, was damaged by an air-launched torpedo that killed and wounded many passengers on board. Would our anti-aircraft guns be adequate to protect us from a similar catastrophe?

That test came sooner than I expected. Suddenly, a Soviet aircraft appeared from the scattered clouds, heading directly toward our ship. It was promptly met by fierce anti-aircraft fire. I could feel the deck under my feet shaking each time the guns fired. The plane circled around the ship and, to our surprise and relief, left without dropping bombs or launching torpedoes. We had been lucky again. But could it possibly have been a reconnaissance flight gathering intelligence for a real attack to follow? Fortunately, our concerns were unwarranted; there were no more contacts with Soviet airplanes and the rest of the sailing was uneventful. We wondered whether the Soviets may have known about the prisoners on board and, thanks to their presence, we were spared. Thus, they may have served as a human shield for us.

After spending the night at sea, we arrived in Danzig (now Gdansk) the next afternoon. Because the port was overcrowded, we couldn't get to the pier until the following morning and had to stay in anchorage for the night. Despite our disappointment about spending another night on the foul-smelling ship, everyone was in high spirits. Although we faced an uncertain future in a foreign land still at war, we were not worried. We felt safe and contented. Finally, we had escaped from the claws of the Red Bear!

12

Danzig, Berlin, and Jena

IT WAS SUNDAY, the first day of October 1944, when we came ashore in Danzig. An early morning chill was still in the air as we stood on the deck and watched the ship navigate through the waterways. The city skyline slowly emerged from the morning mist. In school I had learned that Danzig, like Tallinn, had been one of several port cities on the Hanseatic League's trade route from the thirteenth to the seventeenth century. Before World War II, Danzig had been under Polish control as Gdansk, but it was renamed Danzig during the German occupation. Danzig and its nearby port, Gotenhafen (now Gydinia), were the two major ports on the Baltic Sea for evacuating German troops and Baltic refugees to Germany.

When the ship stopped, we found ourselves docked at a pier in front of a building that looked like a big warehouse. Everyone on board had to wait for the crew's instructions. The prisoners were the first to go ashore. They were the most miserable group of human beings I had ever seen—malnourished, unkempt, and filthy. Those able to walk were marched off the gangplank under the watchful eye of the military guards. The wounded, along with those too weak to walk, were put in a cargo net and hoisted off the ship by a crane, like sacks of potatoes. It was a pitiful sight that made me shudder. How many of them, I wondered, would survive in Germany? I couldn't help thinking of Stephan: how fortunate he had been to live and work on Uncle Karli's farm, where he was treated as a human being. But what had happened to him since? Could he possibly be among those walking off the ship, or is he still in Estonia, captured as a deserter by his former military commanders? In either case, his future seemed grim.

The refugees were next to disembark. We grabbed our baggage and walked down the gangplank. The first thing I noticed was a long table with a sign, "NSF," that identified the women standing behind it. They were members of Nationalsozialistische Frauenschaft (National Socialist Women's League), offering us soup and sandwiches. What a treat! Everything tasted scrumptious after a diet of German Army bread.

After we had finished the last morsel, we moved on to meet the immigration officials. They divided us into two groups. Those who could declare a particular destination in Germany were assigned to the first group, while those with no place to go were placed in the second one. No one wanted to belong to the second group. We knew they would be sent to work in factories producing weapons and ammunition for German fighting forces. Therefore, it was extremely important to get into the first group. That was surprisingly easy; we only had to name an organization or a person who might be able to provide us shelter. During Uncle Haakon's previous stay in Germany, he had been in contact with Grandmother's niece, Mrs. Hilda Oldekop, who was among the last group of Estonians to leave the country after the Soviet takeover in 1940. She lived in Jena, a city in central Germany. Her name and address were sufficient to get us travel permits and train tickets to get there. We also received coupons that allowed us to buy essential food for the next few days.

A special passenger train was waiting for us on a nearby railroad track, scheduled to leave two hours later. Once we were comfortably ensconced in a passenger compartment, I was able to collect my thoughts about past events and ponder the future. Above all, I was thankful to have arrived safely, no longer afraid of being captured by Soviet troops or drowning in the Baltic Sea. I felt enormous gratitude to the men in the Estonian Legion who had slowed the Soviet onslaught long enough for thousands of families to escape while the Wehrmacht was retreating. Without their valiant effort, we certainly wouldn't have been able to escape. But now I faced an uncertain future in a foreign country still at war. How would the German people treat us? How could we find a place to live, and how would my mother be able to make a living for both of us?

My mother believed that the worst nightmare was behind us, and that somehow we would be able to survive until the end of the war. So I stopped worrying and became more sanguine about the future. I had always wanted to visit a foreign country and this was now my opportunity. Not exactly as I had envisioned it as a child—going to Helsinki for the Olympic Games with my father—but a foreign journey, nevertheless. I began to view the future as an adventure, full of new and exciting experiences.

I didn't have to wait long for my first adventure. Once we had found seats on the train, we were allowed to leave it and walk freely around the harbor. A couple of men took advantage of that opportunity and ventured into the immediate neighborhood. Returning minutes later, they announced an exciting discovery: "There is a bar around the corner where they serve cold German beer."

Uncle Haakon and a few others couldn't resist the temptation and decided to join them. German beer was considered the world's best, and what could be a better drink to celebrate our successful escape? Naturally, I wanted to join them—staying behind with the women and children would have been humiliating. Only after Uncle Haakon had assured my mother that he would look after me did I receive her grudging approval.

What a thrill it was for a thirteen-year-old boy to go with men as their equal and explore the wonders of the new world. It was the first time I had been in a bar—everything I saw was new and fascinating. There were a couple of men standing by the bar, and a group of German soldiers drinking and singing at a table in the far corner. I stepped forward and stood proudly in front of the bar with the rest of the men. Uncle Haakon ordered me a nonalcoholic drink that tasted like the mõdu back home, while the other men relished the real stuff. I also got a sip of it from Uncle Haakon's mug, to satisfy my curiosity.

It had a strong, distinctive flavor, quite different from the homemade beer I had tasted on Uncle Karli's farm.

Everyone was in high spirits on the walk back to the train. As we turned the corner, my heart almost stopped. Our train was gone! I could only see the last few cars, about to disappear behind a cluster of trees. "Fast! Let's go," yelled Uncle Haakon. He grabbed my hand and we started to run after the train as if our lives depended on it. I had never run so fast in my life. Fortunately, my practice of the sixty-meter sprint with my classmates at home paid off, and I was able to keep up with the men. But this run was longer than sixty meters— even longer than a hundred meters—and the finish line kept moving away. I knew we could reach it as long as we ran faster than the train. Luckily, the train moved at a steady, slow speed and we were able to reach the last car. The first man to jump on the running board helped the second man to get on board, who in turn helped the next one. We repeated the process until everyone was on board.

As I was gripping a door handle and gasping for breath, someone found an unlocked door. We managed to get inside the car but we were still unable to join the others because the doors between the cars were locked. Meanwhile, I had a chance to calm down and collect my thoughts. I realized how lucky we had been. I was afraid to think what would have happened to us had we left the bar a few minutes later. We probably would have been stranded in Danzig Harbor. Since my mother had all my documents and tickets, I would have been in serious trouble, completely dependent on Uncle Haakon to rescue me from my predicament.

When the train finally came to a stop at Danzig's main station, we were able to join the rest of the families.

"Thank God," my mother shouted when she saw us coming. "We were worried sick. We thought you had missed the train."

"So what happened to you?" Aunt Senta asked.

I decided to remain silent and let Uncle Haakon do the explaining. I thought he did it exceedingly well, but after the initial joy of reunion had worn off, the women started to express their displeasure. My mother was particularly upset. "You were having fun drinking beer while we had to worry about your whereabouts," she complained. I could understand her anguish—the thought of losing her only son in a foreign country amid the chaos of war would be any mother's worst nightmare. I recall hearing a few more angry words about "the terrible grief caused by men's reckless behavior" before everyone finally calmed down.

In late afternoon, our special cars were hooked to a Berlin-bound train, and we left after sundown. Exhausted by the day's events, I fell asleep soon afterward.

Our arrival in Berlin turned out to be disappointing. Instead of entering the bustling railroad station of a major European capital, the train stopped at a small station on the outskirts of the city. The conductor explained that the tracks ahead of us had been damaged by a recent air raid, and we would be taken by buses to the main railroad station for the connecting trains.

As the bus traversed the city streets, I saw the first signs of the effect of Allied air attacks. Several streets were littered with bomb craters and many buildings appeared badly damaged, some practically reduced to rubble. I also saw the twisted wreckage of a British bomber that had been brought down by German anti-aircraft fire, its red, white, and blue roundel still visible on its broken tail. It didn't take me long to realize that civilians in Germany were not spared from the ravages of the war, and that I had just escaped from one war zone into another.

After our arrival at the main station, we learned that the train to Jena would leave at midnight. The trains in Germany traveled at night to avoid becoming targets for Allied air attacks during daylight hours. We had no choice but to wait in the station and be ready to rush for shelter in case of an air raid.

This was Berlin's major train station, probably the famous Hauptbahnhof, with many tracks and platforms. There was also an escalator—the first one I had ever seen. I was fascinated with it because I had just read a magazine article about futuristic people-movers, and here, right in front of my eyes, was a real one, moving people from one floor to the next. Cousin Andres and I got our thrills by repeatedly riding up the escalator and running down the stairs, until our fun was interrupted by the sudden whining of air-raid sirens.

We rushed back to the waiting room and followed directions to the U-Bahn (Underground) station for shelter. There was no panic. Everyone calmly obeyed the instructions of the station wardens. It seemed that the Germans were accustomed to these interruptions in their daily lives. We waited patiently until the "all clear" signal indicated it was safe to return to the main waiting room. Although we did not hear any bomb explosions, the experience left everyone in our group uneasy and jittery. I wondered if these raids were going to be part of our everyday life in Germany.

We spent the rest of the day in the waiting room, and then moved to the platform, well ahead of our departure time. It was teeming with people—an obvious sign that the train was going to be overcrowded. We realized that in order to get seats, we needed to get on the train ahead of the jostling crowd. But that would be very difficult—almost impossible—because of our baggage. Uncle Haakon suggested that one of us should climb through an open window and claim a compartment before the rest of us could arrive with the luggage. I was chosen for the task because I was small enough to slip through the window and was eager to do it. As soon as the train arrived, I was pushed through the window into an empty passenger compartment. A couple of small bags were passed through the window as well. I sat down, spread out the bags and, beaming with pride over my feat, waited for the others to arrive. I waited and waited. I heard a lot of commotion outside, but no one came. Sitting alone in the compartment, I wondered what had happened and waited some more.

The first person to come in was a conductor. He ordered me to leave because the car had been exclusively reserved for mothers with babies and small children. I was crestfallen—my heroic role in the plan had gone awry. By the time I caught up with the rest of my group, all the compartments were jam-packed. We had no choice but to sit on top of our suitcases in a passageway, where we spent a sleepless night until we arrived in Jena just before daybreak.

As we stepped off the train, we were greeted with a sign in large letters, "Jena Paradies Banhof." Aunt Senta noticed it immediately and, with her usual sense of humor, snickered, "Look, we have arrived in paradise. We got nothing to worry about now." But the surroundings belied the meaning of the station sign. A few steps away, a massive windowless concrete structure loomed against the dark sky. The sinister-looking building was an air-raid bunker, a constant reminder of the ever-present danger of air raids. It was dark and the city looked uninviting. This was no paradise.

Things started to look better by the time we arrived at Mrs. Oldekop's apartment. The sight of seven bleary-eyed people with their belongings at her doorstep seemed to startle her, though she had expected us. But she recovered quickly, welcomed us with open arms, prepared breakfast, and rearranged her furniture to accommodate us.

As soon as we had a chance to clean up and catch some sleep, she advised us what we needed to do next. Most urgently, we had to register at the city administration office for food rations. Then we had to exchange our money from the occupation marks to German reichsmarks and find a place to live.

To qualify for food rations, all adults had to have a job or an acceptable reason for not working. Exceptions were made for mothers with small children and in cases where jobs were not available. Since there were no openings for cashiers (my mother's previous position at the pharmacy), both my mother and I received stamps for buying rationed food for one month. The following month we needed to reapply. My mother was relieved, thinking that we could survive with the stamps and whatever money we had until the end of the war.

While searching for a place to live, I discovered that there was a lot to like about Jena. It was a beautiful city on the Saale River, nestled among rolling mountains in the middle of the state of Thuringia. The state was famous for its forests and a centuries-old tradition of sausage-making. The city had a long history, and was the site where Napoleon had fought and defeated the Prussian army. The highly regarded University of Jena had been the home of many famous scientists, philosophers, and poets, including Goethe and

Schiller. Jena was also known for precision machinery, optics, and glass-making. It was the home of the world-famous companies Carl Zeiss Optics and Schott Glass. What we liked most about Jena was that it had been spared the Allied air raids. Being in the heart of Germany, we expected to be safe from ground fighting as well, and we were hopeful we could remain out of danger until Hitler would surrender to the Allied Forces.

My mother and I were fortunate to find a small, furnished one-bedroom apartment in a pleasant residential neighborhood on the east side of the Saale River, an easy walk across the bridge to the city center. Our new home was at Am Kochersgraben 4, a quiet street on a sloping hillside. It was a three-story apartment house that shared a common wall with an adjacent building. Best of all, Aunt Senta's family and Grandmother found a larger apartment a few houses up the hill on the same street.

Our second-floor apartment offered a lovely view of the tree-lined street below. It was adequately furnished in middle-class German style: two beds with nightstands in the bedroom, and a living room with a sofa, a table, and a couple chairs. We also had a small kitchenette. I was surprised to discover that instead of the customary sheets and blankets we had down comforters that looked like deflated balloons sprawled across the beds. When we asked for blankets, the landlady said wryly, "Everyone in Germany sleeps under a *Federbett*. You'll love them when the winter comes." So we had to perspire and suffocate for a while until we learned to appreciate their warmth and coziness on cold winter nights.

Heating fuel and hot water were rationed. The meager amount of kerosene was just adequate for making tea and hot cereal in the morning. Hot water for bathing was available only once a week, when the landlady rolled in a tub large enough for a person to sit in.

The biggest challenge was stretching our food stamps to last through the end of the month. That required a great deal of planning and ingenuity. Every time we bought a loaf of bread, I immediately put scratch marks on the top crust to indicate how much we could eat each day without running out before the end of the month. Dairy products were equally scarce or nonexistent. Instead of butter, we received margarine, and the bluish white liquid, called milk, was available only on certain days.

We were unable to supplement the meager rations with purchases made on the black market as we had done in Estonia, where we'd had our own trusted suppliers. As strangers in a foreign country, we didn't know whom to approach. And even if we had, we would have been afraid of getting caught. The severe punishment for black marketers——a sentence to a concentration camp—seemed to have kept the black market under control. Perhaps that's why the food-distribution system worked so well that we could always buy whatever rationed food we were entitled to. The problem was that there was never enough of it to satisfy my hefty teenage appetite. Hardly a night went by when I didn't go to bed hungry.

We learned quickly that it was unwise to use our meager meat stamps in restaurants, where it was impossible to judge whether we really got the full stamp's worth of meat. Instead, we used the stamps to buy sausages from a butcher. In this way, there was no waste and we received the exact amount to which we were entitled. The divine *Mettwurst* and *Leberwurst* proved that, even in wartime, the Thuringians had not lost their renowned art of sausage-making. Restaurants, however, were good for ordering dishes that did not require stamps. Those daily specials, called *Stammgerichte*, were vegetarian dishes consisting of potatoes and whatever vegetables happened to be in season. For a more nourishing meal we had to surrender five or ten gram's worth of fat stamps.

We were shocked to learn that foreigners, called *Ausländer*, were permitted to eat in restaurants only after 2 p.m. By that time, however, the *Stammgerichte* and other popular dishes were usually gone. Fortunately, many restaurant owners ignored that regulation. With Uncle Haakon's fluent German we were able to get into most restaurants in town at any time of the day. Our favorite was a cozy midtown restaurant called Zum Klause. Its owners served generous portions (a very important consideration) of well-prepared food at reasonable prices and always treated us cordially. The waiters were mostly Romanians who, having been forced to leave their homeland, shared a plight similar to ours. I remember a tall, dark Romanian with a bushy mustache who adored little Marike and loved to spoil her with candy.

In Zum Klause we happened to meet other Estonians, who introduced us to their informal gatherings in Café Sonne across the street. It was a spacious, old fashioned café that served coffee and cakes topped with a saccharin-sweetened foamy substance, which we jokingly called soapsuds. The coffee, of course, was not real. It was ersatz, made of roasted barley, and was commonly called *Mukifuki* (short for mocca faux). The café was a great place to linger after dinner and mingle with other Estonians who had found their way to Jena. Uncle Haakon was delighted to run into his old friend Reverend Friedrich Stockholm, the former pastor of Saint Charles Church in Tallinn, who immediately invited us to his Sunday services at a local Lutheran church.

Another gathering place for the Estonians in Jena was a clubhouse named Schnapphans. We went there regularly on Saturdays to meet our countrymen and share information about friends and relatives. Who had managed to escape? Who was left behind? Who had lost their lives crossing the Baltic Sea? What were Estonians doing in various cities and towns in Germany? A good source of information was a weekly Estonian-language newspaper, Eesti Sõna (Estonian Word), published in Berlin. When Uncle Haakon became the distributor for the paper in Jena, he asked me if I would like to sell it at our Saturday meetings. Without blinking an eye, I accepted the offer. It was my very first job—a wonderful way to escape the everyday tedium and earn some pocket money. Every Saturday, I set up a newsstand at the entrance to the meeting room. It consisted of two chairs—one for the stack of paper, the other for a shoebox where I kept the money. I loved the job, met a lot of people, and walked home with a pocketful of small cash—the money that I had earned all by myself. There was no need to ask my mother for an allowance any more.

Shortly after arriving in Jena, my mother and I had a discussion about my education. Since I had completed Estonian elementary school, I should have enrolled immediately in the local German Gymnasium. But I hesitated because school had already started a month earlier and I didn't consider myself fluent enough in German to keep up with the studies. I was also concerned that, having seen the boys from the nearby Gymnasium strutting raucously in their Hitler Youth uniforms, I would be an outsider in that crowd and might even become a victim of bullying.

So we decided to hold off on formal schooling until the inevitable collapse of the Nazi regime, which we expected to happen long before the end of the school year. Meanwhile, I decided to take private lessons to improve my German. My mother found an Estonian lady, Miss Kaasik, who was willing to offer semi-private lessons to me and Maie Teene, whose family also had settled in Jena. We met at the teacher's apartment three times a week and worked on regular homework assignments. It was a refreshing change from an otherwise boring teenage existence.

My mother decided it was time to prepare for the eventuality that we may have to remain in Germany indefinitely. She enrolled in a typing class at the local secretarial school, thinking that typing would be a basic skill for any female office worker. She attended classes faithfully during the day and practiced diligently during evening hours. The fact that we didn't have a typewriter didn't bother her at all; a cardboard keyboard was good enough for doing her finger exercises. Her diligence and determination paid off when she got a full-time secretarial position after the war ended.

The adjustment to life in Jena went rather well, thanks to Mrs. Oldekop's helpful support and advice. She introduced us to the city and showed us many interesting places. On her recommendation, we became members of the City Library, a rich source of information to feed my hunger for learning. I spent hours studying the map of Germany, not only to learn its geography, but to track the progress of the Allied forces, hoping for faster advances on the western front than on the eastern. On one occasion, Mrs. Oldekop took us to the Zeiss Planetarium, the oldest planetarium in the world and the pride of the city. I recall a memorable afternoon spent marveling at the movement of the planets and stars projected on its dome-shaped screen.

But most importantly, Mrs. Oldekop showed us ways to supplement our meager food rations. She took us to the countryside, where we could buy fresh fruit and vegetables directly from farmers for a fraction of the price in the city. I recall a day when we went with her to a farm in a nearby village to buy freshly harvested apples and pears. As we filled our bags, the farmer offered each of us a small purple plum and asked, "Why don't you try my *Zwetschgen*?"

It was delicious—sweet, juicy, and slightly tart. Mrs. Oldekop explained that they were actually Italian prune plums that were widely cultivated in the region. She said, "They are good for eating just like this and they are also good for baking tarts."

"The season will be over soon," the farmer advised.

"Don't buy too many," Mrs. Oldekop cautioned my mother. "On the way back, the highway is lined with *Zwetschgen* trees. There we are allowed to harvest the fruit that has fallen on the ground for free."

We followed her good advice and filled our bags, while munching the delicious plums at the same time. The following weekend, we borrowed her four-wheel utility cart, called a *weggele* by the locals, and went back to buy more apples and collect the last of the roadside harvest. Back home, we gorged ourselves on these fruits endlessly, regardless of how many nocturnal bathroom visits we had to make.

The apples and plums were not the only things that interrupted our sleep at night. Several nights a week we were awakened by air-raid sirens and had to rush to the shelter in the basement. Soon it became a regular nightly ritual, as Jena was on the flight path for the British bombers on their way to industrial targets in the Halle-Merseburg area. After a while, we became less fearful of the threat but grew more annoyed at the disruption of our sleep. It was hard to leave the comfort of the warm *Federbett*, dress, and run downstairs to join our neighbors in the shelter. Usually we just sat there quietly, tried to nap to the sound of a few hushed voices, and waited for the "all clear" signal before going back to bed.

One thing I learned quickly after stepping on German soil was that I had to be careful greeting people in public places, where the obligatory salute was *Heil Hitler*. I tried to avoid saying it, but had to be cautious deciding when to use that greeting and when an old-fashioned *Guten Morgen* or *Guten Tag* would suffice. To avoid any problems, I always let the shopkeeper greet me first so that I could respond in kind, depending on which salutation he used. With the end of the war so close, there was no need to get into trouble with the Nazi authorities.

13

Surviving Allied Bomb Attacks

WITH THE ARRIVAL of winter, life became more difficult. Soon after we had depleted our extra fall fruit supplies, we began to understand the real meaning of hunger. The frigid weather also brought more gloom. Our apartment received some heat in the morning, but it was barely enough to keep us warm throughout the day. At night we thanked the Germans for their *Federbetten*, which kept us warm in our beds. But when the nightly air raids became more frequent, we were forced to spend more and more time in the cold basement shelter. Despite intense war propaganda that insisted otherwise, there were signs that the inevitable defeat of Germany was not far away.

Passing a large military hospital on our way downtown, we saw ambulances come and go more frequently. There were also more ambulatory patients with severe battlefield injuries on the streets around the hospital. Men with missing limbs and burned or disfigured faces made the horrors of war palpable to everyone in the city. I wondered why so many men had to sacrifice themselves for the follies of a couple of dictators.

Every time I crossed the bridge across Saale River, I noticed groups of teenage boys in bluish-gray uniforms, only a couple of years older than I, stationed alongside the bridge. They were the *Luftwaffenhelfer* (Air Force helpers), whose job was to protect the bridge from air attacks. They activated smoke generators at the first warning to camouflage the bridge, and they controlled huge balloons attached to steel cables to fend off low-flying aircraft. On cold days the smoke lingered for hours before it dissipated. I recall several occasions when I crossed the bridge with a handkerchief over my mouth and nose to prevent choking by the noxious gas.

The sight of military units marching on the streets of Jena became more common as time went by. One afternoon my eye caught something unusual—a military column that bore no resemblance to the orderly strut of the Wehrmacht. Clad in shabby military garb with no insignia, these men walked in a casual way, flanked by rifle-carrying German soldiers. I thought that they were prisoners of war, but somehow they looked very different than the Russian prisoners whom I saw in Danzig. These men appeared relatively healthy and in good spirits, compared to the wretched Russians. Suddenly, it dawned on me that they were American and British soldiers and bomber pilots captured by the Germans. It seemed the prisoners from the western front were treated more humanely, much as I imagined the Americans and British probably treated their captured German soldiers.

Our Christmas in Jena was a sad one. We had planned to visit Grandmother and Aunt Senta's family for a Christmas Eve dinner. We were looking forward to moments of joy in the midst of a gloomy world. We still had a can of Estonian ham that my mother had saved for this occasion, and Grandmother prepared various salads to go with it. When my mother opened the can, we discovered that the ham was spoiled because of a leaky seal. What a disaster! Everyone was shocked and deeply disappointed. My mother was particularly distraught. "This is terrible," she moaned. "Imagine, I carried this heavy can in my suitcase all the way from Estonia. I could have brought something more valuable instead."

We didn't have a Christmas tree, but Aunt Senta had bought a few candles and pine twigs to remind us that it was Christmas. This was the first Christmas away from our homeland. Our thoughts and prayers went to the relatives and friends who had been left behind or sent to unknown destinations in Siberia. I couldn't help but think how lucky we were to be among those who were able to escape and celebrate Christmas together with the remaining few of our family. We sang some Christmas songs, exchanged a few small gifts, and watched the gleam in my young cousins' eyes as they unwrapped their presents. Then we sat down to have the salads that Grandmother had prepared to go with the ham. But without the ham, the meal left us hungry and dissatisfied—it was not the Christmas Eve dinner we had hoped for. We all agreed to have a real Christmas dinner on Christmas Day at our much-loved Zum Klause restaurant.

As we arrived early, at noon, our favorite waiter seated us at a comfortable corner table. A few Christmas decorations, scattered around the dining room, reminded us that it was Christmas. We decided to splurge and spend our precious meat stamps for a meal fit for the occasion. The holiday special on the menu was roast pork, a traditional Estonian Christmas food. I couldn't remember the last time I had tasted it. My mouth began to water. But noticing that it called for 100 grams' worth of meat stamps—almost one-tenth of my monthly allowance—I hesitated. My mother, however, insisted on ordering it. "Don't worry about the stamps," she said. "Your body needs meat to grow. Remember, it's Christmas." So I ordered, ruefully watching her surrender two fifty-gram meat stamps to the waiter.

It was a magnificent meal—a tender slice of pork soaked in gravy and served with roasted potatoes and sauerkraut. I relished it until the last morsel was scraped off the plate. Everyone at the table savored the meal as well. We all were in high spirits, and the canned-ham disaster seemed like ancient history.

As we were leaving the restaurant, I felt slightly nauseous. I asked others to wait for me and rushed to the restroom. I arrived just in time to drop my entire dinner into the toilet bowl. After many months on a near-starvation diet, my stomach was unable to digest such a rich meal. What a calamity, I thought. A total waste of my precious stamps.

The arrival of the New Year did not bring much change to our daily lives. The nightly air-raid sirens warning us to find shelter had become almost routine. They were deemed more a nuisance than a warning of danger. Everyone thought that Jena, being on the flight path of bombers heading toward industrial targets past our city, would be spared the deadly bombs. Dresden, a major city about a hundred miles east of Jena, had been similarly safe from the Allied air raids. Therefore, we weren't the least bit concerned when Uncle Haakon announced that he was going to Dresden to help Estonians who had fled there from the Soviet Army, which was advancing through Poland and Czechoslovakia.

He was still in Dresden when we heard the news that the city had suffered a massive air attack. While the details about the attack were sketchy, we were afraid that the damage may have been actually more extensive than officially reported. Rumors were circulating that a ferocious firestorm had swept through the city. With no news from Uncle Haakon, we started to suspect the worst. Had he been caught in the attack? Was he dead or alive? My mother and I went to see Aunt Senta to comfort and support her and the children in their anxiety. There was nothing more we could do but wait and pray.

Two days later, Uncle Haakon came home. He was limping, and his unshaven face and overcoat were smeared with traces of soot and ashes. "I was lucky to survive," he said. "The whole city was burning when I got out of the shelter. The buildings around me were in flames and the heat was unbearable. I could hardly breathe."

He paused for a moment and then continued, "I wet my hat, coat, and scarf in a fountain and I tried to run away from the flames, but they were all around me. Finally, I saw a stone wall in the distance, pulled the coat over my head, and made a dash toward it. I climbed up on the wall and jumped to the other side. That's how I sprained my ankle."

Disturbed by his story, we wondered whether a similar air raid could shatter our relatively tranquil life in Jena as well. A month later we received the answer.

It was a clear day on March 19, 1945. My mother and I had just completed some errands in town and were ready for midday dinner. We walked by a traditional German restaurant, the name of which I can't recall, and she said, "We have passed this restaurant many times, but have never eaten here. Let's try it."

The centuries-old building had a marvelous dining room, which emanated a relaxed and warm atmosphere. It seemed a perfect place for a leisurely meal. We had barely been seated when the air-raid sirens started to blast their warning. "What an odd time for an air raid, in the middle of the day," my mother commented.

The diners were directed to the bomb shelter in the restaurant's basement. For some unknown reason, my mother hesitated, grabbed my arm, and said, "This is an old building. I don't know how safe the shelter is. The big city bunker is only a few minutes from here. If we hurry, we can still get there safely." I agreed instantly because I had heard that the underground bunker was the biggest and strongest one in the city.

We started our race towards the shelter at a brisk walk, but by the time we joined the stream of people heading toward the bunker, we were running. Old men, working as air-raid wardens, kept the crowd moving down the stairs and through a huge steel door. I had never been inside that shelter before. It was divided into several rooms filled with wooden benches. The walls were covered with emergency instructions and propaganda posters. We followed the flow of people until we found a place to settle down. There were people of all walks of life—old men and women, young women with babies and children. As I was looking around for a familiar face, I spotted Reverend Stockholm with his wife, beckoning us to join them. It was comforting to have a man of the cloth with us at a time like that.

Moments later, I heard the distant rumble of the first explosions. As the menacing sound of exploding bombs grew louder and more frequent, I realized that this was no overflight—this time Jena was the target of attack.

Suddenly a crescendo of explosions shook the walls of the bunker, and the lights went out. The breathless silence was broken only by a baby's cry and Reverend Stockholm's hushed prayer. I was also praying, hoping and praying that the underground bunker would be strong enough to protect us. In the candlelight I could see only shadows of bodies crouched over in silence.

Our agony ended when the rumble of explosions subsided and we heard the sound of the "all clear" signal. We still had to wait for the debris to be cleared from the exit before we could leave the bunker.

Our first sight on the way out was truly shocking. The neighborhood I had known before was no longer there. Several buildings around the bunker had been reduced to rubble. The devastation was unbelievable. A few steps away, I saw the body of a dead man with streaks of clotted blood covering his pale face. The air was full of dust and smoke. We tried to find our way out of the clutter and confusion and looked for streets that were still passable.

I hoped that the bridge would be undamaged so that we could cross the river. And what about our apartment? I wondered. Is it still there? Maybe it had been destroyed like so many other buildings around us In that case, where could we find shelter in the middle of winter? All these frightening questions raced through my mind as we made our way toward the bridge.

I began to breathe easier when I saw the bridge intact and open to foot traffic. As we crossed the bridge, the thought of losing our home still kept haunting me. The distant row of buildings across the river appeared undamaged. We passed the hospital and walked up the hill toward our street. With no signs of bomb damage, we became more encouraged; the neighborhood apparently had been spared. When we reached the corner of our street, we stopped. We stood for a moment and stared at our building. It was an incredible relief to see it looking exactly as it had that morning, when we'd left. As we crossed the doorway and entered our small, sparsely furnished apartment, my mother and I hugged each other. Thank God, we still had a roof over our heads.

Our next concern was the safety of Grandmother and Aunt Senta's family. They had recently moved to a bigger apartment closer to the center of the city, and we were seriously concerned about their survival. It turned out that they were safe, but had lived through some harrowing moments. Aunt Senta and her children were on the way to the basement shelter when the first barrage of bombs exploded near the building. The large glass windows along the stairs shattered and sent a shower of splinters through the stairway. Miraculously, they survived with only minor cuts and scrapes. Their building itself survived without major damage.

However, Aunt Senta suffered serious injury later that evening. Stepping into the darkness of her bathroom—the whole city was without electric power—she scratched the cornea of her eye on the corner of a glass shelf. I was stuck by the irony of it; she had survived the most perilous moments of the attack, only to be injured in the quiet aftermath.

It took days to determine the full extent of the destruction in the wake of the bombing. The central part of the city had been hit particularly hard. The buildings on the street of our favorite restaurant, Zum Klause, had been reduced to rubble. The most shocking discovery was that the restaurant where my mother and I had been going to dine that day had collapsed from a direct bomb hit. Everyone in the basement shelter had been buried alive. That news sent shivers down my spine. We would have been among those victims had we not decided to follow my mother's instinct and gone instead to the big bunker. Luck had saved us again!

This harrowing experience convinced us to join the many residents of Jena leaving the city for safer destinations. We had been in contact with Uncle Karli, who had found a job as a miller near Bad Berka, a small rural town about fifteen miles west of Jena. He urged us to join him there, to be safe from future bomb attacks. It seemed an ideal place—no one would drop bombs on a small farming town—and we immediately accepted his invitation. Grandmother was particularly happy about the idea. "It is very important for the family to be together in these uncertain times," she said. So we packed our few belongings and left the battered city.

Bad Berka, a small town surrounded by farms and forests, was a huge contrast to Jena. The nearest city was Weimar, the birthplace of the Weimar Republic following the First World War. We found nice ac-

commodations in Bergern, a small village a couple of miles north of
Bad Berka. My mother and I were able to rent a room from a lady
whose husband was in the army, fighting on the Eastern front. Our
room was a spacious second-floor loft with simple country-style fur-
nishings. The beds came with traditional Federbetten, just like in
Jena. Grandmother and Aunt Senta's family found larger accommodations a few houses away.

Tranquil country living, being awakened by a rooster's crow
instead of air-raid sirens, was exactly what we needed. I will never
forget my first night there. The silence was still broken by the familiar
roar of a bomber fleet flying above us, but this time there were no air-
raid sirens, no clacking sound of anti-aircraft fire, just the droning of
aircraft propellers. There was no need to jump out of bed and rush to
shelter. I listened for a while and then rolled over comfortably under
my warm feather quilt. It was pure bliss to continue sleeping, knowing that we were securely out of harm's way.

A week or two later, we received a letter from Mrs. Oldekop in-
forming us of another air attack on Jena. She noted that our previous
neighborhood had suffered extensive damage and that the building
attached to ours had received a direct bomb hit. "Thank God, we left
Jena just in time," my mother commented when she read the letter.

Another important advantage of living in farm country was that
food was more readily available than in Jena. We could always get
fresh vegetables—turnips, kohlrabi, and carrots—from local farmers.
We also came to appreciate the advantage of living near Uncle Karli,
who supplied us with flour and oatmeal from the mill so that we could
enjoy porridge or pancakes for breakfast, or barter the grains for a
couple of fresh eggs.

We found Bergern the ideal place to hide until the end of the war,
which we expected to happen any day. As Hitler became more desperate, he began to recruit teenagers as young as sixteen, or even
fifteen years of age. Since my fourteenth birthday was soon approaching, my mother began to worry that even I might to fall into the
hands of aggressive recruiting officers. So I had to keep a low profile.
I stayed home and avoided walking alone on main streets and in pub-

lic places. I hated being confined, but I complied with my mother's wishes and hoped that the Americans would arrive soon.

14

The Americans Are Coming

THE DAY WE had been waiting for arrived sooner than we expected. It did not happen as I had imagined it—with the roar of tanks and blasts of cannon fire. It came unexpectedly and peacefully on a beautiful spring day. Uncle Haakon and I were returning from a walk in the field when, suddenly, almost out of nowhere, two small military vehicles approached us. There were two more a short distance behind them. Their olive-green color made them blend perfectly into the surrounding vegetation. The soldiers on board were armed with automatic weapons and their helmets and uniforms looked different than any others I had seen before. They stopped almost directly in front of us. Uncle Haakon glanced at them and said to me, "They must be Americans. Stay here while I go and talk to them."

As they were talking, several villagers gathered around me, keeping a suspicious distance from the vehicles. After a brief discussion, Uncle Haakon returned and translated the message from the soldiers. "It's the American Army," he said. "They have arrived here. Their main forces are just behind the hill. They asked me to tell you to turn in any weapons and cameras you may have. The regular forces are coming tomorrow morning. They plan to enter peacefully, but in case of armed resistance, the village will be leveled by artillery fire."

After being assured that there were no weapons or Wehrmacht units in the village, the soldiers jumped into their jeeps and drove away. They disappeared into the field just as quietly and quickly as they had arrived, leaving only a cloud of dust behind.

Uncle Haakon cautioned me to hide any signs of joy from the villagers because he didn't know how they would react to this surprising turn of events. Although they appeared calm and unemotional, we had no idea how many true Nazis were among them. We had always scrupulously avoided discussing politics with the locals.

The whole family was elated when we brought home the good news. "Thank God, the Americans got here before the Russians," Grandmother exclaimed, expressing everyone's feeling of immense relief and liberation.

"But we still have to be careful," my mother cautioned. "What if some militant Nazis hear that you welcomed the Americans? They may come for a reprisal against us." The thought that this could actually happen curbed our joy for the rest of the evening. I was sleepless throughout the night, ecstatic about the arrival of the Americans while still fearing for Uncle Haakon's safety. Fortunately, the only known Nazi party members, the landowners of a nearby estate, had disappeared days before, and the night passed uneventfully.

We were up early the next morning, eagerly awaiting the arrival of American troops. We had almost finished our breakfast when I heard a soft cracking sound outside. I walked to the window and was startled by a helmet-wearing American soldier peeking into our kitchen. Farther behind him, a group of soldiers was going from house to house, looking inside each one. I couldn't believe my ears how quietly they moved. Accustomed to the marching sound of the spiked boots of the German and Russian armies, I was stunned by the quiet movement of the Americans in their rubber-soled boots.

From the second-floor window I saw artillery units taking up position on a nearby hill with their guns pointing toward Bad Berka. Uncle Haakon went out to chat with the soldiers, who were delighted to find someone with a good command of English. They told him that the remnants of the German Army in Bad Berka had been given an ultimatum to surrender, and they were waiting for their response. They didn't have to wait long. At the first sight of white flags, the soldiers moved on to take control of Bad Berka, leaving only a small cadre behind.

I always remember the events of that happy day—April 12, 1945—as if they happened only yesterday. For us, it was the day we had been waiting for since our arrival in Germany. It was the dawn of what would be a new chapter in our lives, one that hopefully would be happier and more peaceful.

We noticed the first sign of the new era the very next day, when a sudden deluge of milk appeared on the village square. Since the dairy farmers were unable to transport their uninterrupted milk production to the stores, they had brought their entire cache to the village square and poured it freely for anyone who came with an empty bucket. The milk was fresh and creamy, utterly unlike the thin, bluish liquid to which we had become accustomed. The village square was full of excitement as smiling women and children rushed back and forth with their mugs and jugs. My mother made sure that we took full advantage of this unexpected cornucopia. I remember drinking so much milk that she had to slow me down by reminding me of the sad experience with my pork roast on Christmas Day.

Another noticeable change was increased traffic on the nearby highway. There was a massive eastward movement of American Army vehicles delivering troops and supplies to the front, where the fighting was still going on. Waving to bystanders, the victorious-looking soldiers were friendly and jovial, as if they had already won the war. I was truly impressed by their generosity to children. They showered them with chocolates and candy, something that I had never seen an occupying army do before. They were particularly generous to foreigners like us, who were in Germany as refugees or forced laborers from German-occupied territories. To gain the soldiers' attention and favor, we wore ribbons with Estonian tricolors on our lapels and flaunted them proudly, as did other refugees. I was amazed by the multitude of national colors on display. It was like a miniature United Nations, with Latvian, Lithuanian, Polish, Hungarian, Romanian, and various other flags. The Poles were particularly proud to display their national colors after being forced by the Nazis to wear the humiliating Polish letter "P" patch. The ribbons also helped us find other Estonian families living in the area.

Yet another striking change was a great increase in the air traffic above us. In addition to American bombers flying at high altitude toward their targets, there were many transport planes and other small aircraft buzzing at lower altitudes. It took a little while to get used to the idea that they were friendly aircraft and that there was no need to run for cover. For weeks, Cousin Andres still ran for cover at the first whir of aircraft propellers; his harrowing experience in Jena had left him with an automatic reaction to the sound of any airplane.

We took long walks in the nearby forests and enjoyed the flowers that were starting to blossom in the fields. I discovered a shortcut to the highway leading to Bad Berka, which made visiting Uncle Karli faster than traveling by the main road. It involved hiking on a steep trail through a forest, in the shade of spruce and pine trees. When I was hiking with Uncle Haakon, we were always on the lookout for objects that had been abandoned by the retreating German Army. We didn't have much use for military equipment, but one day we stumbled on a real treasure. Hidden behind bushes, there was a neatly wrapped canvas bag that contained a blue-gray German air force officer's uniform. It was in excellent condition, almost brand new, made of high-quality fabric. "It must have been discarded by a deserting Luftwaffe officer," Uncle Haakon remarked. The tight-fitting jacket seemed too small for Uncle Haakon, so he handed it to me and said, "You try it on. I shouldn't be wearing it, but you can. You are too young to be accused of being a Luftwaffe officer." It was a good fit, only slightly oversized. "It's yours," Uncle Haakon said. "You'll grow into it in no time. Grandmother will remove the insignia and make the necessary alterations." Since I was starting to outgrow the clothes I had brought from home, I considered it a perfect gift for my forthcoming birthday. Serendipitously, I had become the proud owner of an outfit that kept me warm and well dressed for several years.

Food, particularly meat, was still scarce. When Uncle Karli heard us complain about it, he suggested that we get a few Estonian families together so that we could afford to buy a whole pig directly from a local farmer. He would then slaughter it and divide the meat among us.

"I know some farmers around here who might be willing to sell," Uncle Karli said. "As a former farmer, I know how to butcher pigs."

We had no problem finding families wanting to join us. The mere thought of pork roast was enough to make everyone salivate. Uncle Karli took a *weggele* from the mill and, together with Uncle Haakon and a couple of other men, left on a shopping expedition. I tagged along in the hope of finding some excitement.

We did find a farmer willing to give up one of his prized pigs for the price we offered, but just when the deal seemed closed, the farmer said he needed a permit to sell the pig.

"Where can we get the permit?" Uncle Haakon asked.

"It used to be the village administrator, but he has disappeared. There is no one in charge now."

"The Americans are in charge now," Uncle Haakon said. "We need to get it from the army."

"If they issue an official permit, it's a deal," said the farmer.

We found an army unit in a nearby building, but instead of Americans, we met Belgian soldiers who had been fighting alongside the American forces. When they heard our request, they broke out in laughter.

"The farmer wants what?" asked one soldier. "A permit to sell a pig? Doesn't he know that this is a war? His pigs could have been killed or lost during the fighting without any permits."

Another soldier, equally amused, added, "We don't even know how to write one."

"If I dictate the text for you, would you be willing to type and sign one?" Uncle Haakon asked. "We are hungry and one pig can feed many families."

The officer in charge agreed, typed the permit, signed, and sealed it with a stamp. Then he punched an additional stamp on it. "Just in case, to make it look more official," he chuckled and wished us good luck. The soldiers were still laughing when we walked away with the prized permit.

The farmer was impressed by the official-looking document and the deal was closed. I didn't see the slaughter because I was sent home with a message for our women to rush out and buy as much salt as possible before the stores closed for the day (most stores sold only a small amount of goods at a time to a customer). Salt was the only preservative at that time since refrigeration was not yet available.

We had the most fabulous feast that evening. Our meal was truly beyond lavish and joyful. We gorged on pork and celebrated by toasting, singing, and dancing. We rejoiced that our wishes had finally come true. The Americans had reached us before the Russians, there was no more fighting around us, and the end of the war was near.

We waited eagerly for the inevitable German surrender and the official end of the war. I was hoping it would come to pass on my fourteenth birthday, but to my disappointment, it did not happen. I had to wait two more days. On May 8, 1945, we received the news that Germany had surrendered. The war in Europe was over. Turbulent times were finally behind us. We believed that a much brighter future lay ahead, and we looked forward to it with confidence and hope.

15

Time to Flee Again

THE WAR IN Europe was over. The German Army had been defeated and the country was in a shambles. Germany had been divided into zones by the four occupying powers: American, British, French, and Russian. Each zone was under the control of its respective military command, which tried to maintain law and order under enormously chaotic conditions.

We began to wonder what the future would hold for us. Millions of refugees of many nationalities were scattered across Germany. Displaced by the war in one way or another, we later became known as "Displaced Persons" (DPs). Some were able to return to their home countries, but for people from the Baltics, who had already suffered more than enough under communism, that was not an option. Having barely managed to escape the horrors of another Soviet occupation, going back was unthinkable.

Anxiety about our future was heightened by a lack of reliable information. Frightening rumors about resettling all refugees in their native countries were constantly floating around. The Polish laborers in our village had already left for their homeland, but not before ransacking the villa of the landowner who had employed them. Would we be forced to return to Russian-occupied Estonia as well? Although we couldn't imagine such a horrifying turn of events, we decided to become better informed so that we could protect our interests.

Uncle Haakon went to the regional U.S. Army headquarters in Weimar to find out how well the Americans understood the quandary of Baltic refugees and what they planned to do with us. He returned with both good and bad news.

"First of all," he said, "we don't have to worry about being sent back to Estonia. The Americans understand that we can't go back. No one is even talking about forced repatriation. I told them that if they did that, the Russians would have us on the first train to Siberia."

"Thank God, we don't have to worry about that anymore," my mother said with a sigh of relief.

"But I also have bad news," Uncle Haakon added. "The officers told me that they plan to withdraw American troops from Thuringia. It will become part of the Russian Zone."

"Oh, no!" Aunt Senta gasped. "This is where we live now." Shaking her head in disbelief, she moaned, "I can't believe that the Americans are so stupid. They went all the way to the Czechoslovakian border and now they are giving all this land to the Russians."

"You are right," Uncle Haakon agreed, "but this had already been decided in Yalta by Roosevelt, Churchill, and Stalin."

"When will all this happen?" my mother asked. "And where can we go?"

"The Russians are expected to be here by the first of July," said Uncle Haakon. "I told the Americans that we needed to get out of here before that happens. They understood that. They also said they want to evacuate us along with the army. But they made no promises. They recommended that we move to Weimar, where they have temporary housing for those who want to be evacuated. They will even send trucks to help us move."

"So, let's not wait," my mother suggested. "Let's go to Weimar as soon as we can."

We packed our few belongings, and on the day when the truck came, we bid farewell to our kind and generous landlady. She was waiting for her husband's return from the eastern front, but with no news from him, she worried that he might have been killed or captured by the Soviet Army. She was not alone. There were countless people all over Europe who were desperately looking for their relatives and loved ones lost in the whirlwind of war.

"It is too early. There is still hope," my mother consoled her. We thanked our landlady and then left for Weimar, picking up Uncle Karli, Aunt Olli, and a few other Estonians along the way.

In Weimar, the U.S. Army had set up a temporary camp in a school building, with rows of bunk beds in every classroom. The accommodations offered hardly any privacy. The best we could do was to find a group of bunks together in a corner of a second-floor room and hang up a sheet to separate us from the others. The beds were a bit uncomfortable, but I was happy to have a whole bed to myself, and not have to share it as I did in Kallemäe.

It was a great relief to everyone that we no longer had to worry about food. We received our daily meals from the military kitchen in the next-door building. The food was adequate and no one was hungry anymore. There was not much to do other than settle down and wait for the next move.

Weimar was a sleepy, provincial city. Once a cultural center and home to German literary icons Goethe and Schiller, as well as the composers Liszt and Brahms, it had suffered significant destruction from Allied air attacks. Many buildings and historic sites had been destroyed or damaged. The city was bustling with American troops in trucks and jeeps who navigated their way through the wreckage on rubble-filled streets. I hardly saw any soldiers walk or march in formation as the Germans or Russians did. The Americans seemed to prefer traveling by motor vehicle, driving their jeeps for distances even as short as a city block, always with a foot dangling to the side. A curious observer once commented that they even went to the outhouse on a jeep. He was not joking; I actually saw some soldiers in a building next to ours drive to the toilets across a courtyard.

When they were not racing their jeeps, they were almost always throwing a small white ball to each other. I heard that it was used in a game called baseball, played on a large field where the players hit this ball with a bat and then ran through several bases in order to reach home base. It seemed similar to *laptuu*, the game I used to play with a tennis ball at school in Estonia. Seeing how much skill and enthusiasm went into their throwing and catching of the ball, I came to the conclusion that baseball must be, without doubt, America's favorite sport. I also couldn't help noticing that whenever they threw the ball, they chewed gum at the same time. I don't think I ever saw an American soldier whose jaws weren't in a perpetual grinding motion. Their gum-chewing habit was perhaps the most widely adopted custom that American soldiers brought to Europe.

The massive presence of American troops in Weimar included many black soldiers. Most of us had seen black people in movies, but never in person. Although I had seen a black man previously in Jena, I was still, as were most Europeans, fascinated by men of different skin color than mine.

Perhaps one reason Weimar had such a large contingent of American soldiers was its proximity to the former Buchenwald concentration camp. It was only four miles north of the city. We first learned about its existence from the newspapers, after it had been discovered and made public by the U.S. Army. I don't know how many local residents had been aware of it; it certainly wasn't something they would have talked about in public, particularly with foreigners. We knew that concentration camps existed in Germany—many Estonians had been sent there as well—but we didn't know that we had lived so near one of them. I found it hard to believe that such atrocities had taken place in our vicinity. The inmates—Jews, gypsies, criminals, and political prisoners from many of the German-controlled territories—had been released by the U.S. Army and now roamed the streets of Weimar like walking skeletons. Some foraged for food, while others sought revenge on their former prison guards. They were in immensely worse condition than the Russian prisoners of war I had seen walking down the gangplank in Danzig. Seeing these hollow-eyed, emaciated bodies in tattered clothes made such a profound impression on me that I was unable to sleep for several weeks. I was glad that the war had ended their nightmare and that the perpetrators were being brought to justice. They made me think of my father and the millions of others who still languished in the Soviet Gulags in Siberia. Who would liberate them? The world had gotten rid of one awful dictator, but the other was still in power, continuing to commit crimes against humanity.

Uncle Haakon visited army headquarters almost daily, hoping to bring back good news, but each visit ended in disappointment. It was always the same story: the army still intended to evacuate us, but was unable provide a firm schedule. Our anxiety grew with each day of waiting, as the deadline for transferring power to the Soviets was approaching fast. We didn't want to wait until the last moment, as we had done in Estonia, so we decided to take charge of our own future. Uncle Haakon found a local truck owner who was willing to take us out of Thuringia. We gathered a few Estonians who were equally anxious to leave and were willing to share the cost. Each family con-tributed some valuables that hadn't been already bartered away—a silver spoon or a gold ring—to meet the driver's exorbitant demand.

Still, one problem remained. We had no gasoline. Throughout Germany, there was a severe shortage of gas for civilian use. How-ever, the military seemed to have an unlimited supply. Our driver thought that we would have more success than a German citizen in dealing with the army. Therefore, several men and I, under Uncle Haakon's leadership, went to a U.S. Army motor pool in the hope of getting the necessary fuel for our escape.

The motor pool was staffed almost exclusively by black troops. A few soldiers gathered around us and listened intently as Uncle Haakon explained where we came from, why we had to leave, and why we needed to buy gas. The only question was what to offer them? Reichsmarks were practically worthless and the only trading "currencies" at the time—cigarettes and alcohol—were of no interest to the soldiers. They had plenty of cigarettes and more premium Scotch and Irish whiskey than they could ever drink. They were only interested in meeting white, young women—preferably blondes. They probably would have traded away nearly any vehicle from the motor pool for a few blonde girls. For obvious reasons, we were unable to meet their request and we left empty-handed.

As we were passing the rows of parked trucks on the way out, one of our men noticed the five-gallon gas tanks strapped to the side of each vehicle.

"Look at these gas cans!" he exclaimed. "A few of these would be enough to get us out of here. I don't think the soldiers would miss them much. They have plenty of gas."

"I didn't see any guards around. Why don't we wait until dark and appropriate a few cans?" suggested another.

Everyone agreed without blinking an eye. This was not the time to worry about ethics or getting caught, when the lives of our families were at stake.

As soon the sun had set, we returned to the motor pool, found the trucks still unguarded, and carried out our devious mission. Each man, including myself, grabbed a can and made a quick getaway to a prearranged meeting point with our driver. That was the only time I had ever stolen something, but somehow I didn't feel a trace of guilt or shame. On the contrary, I was proud to perform a heroic act of helping desperate families escape from the looming Soviet threat. Thinking about it in retrospect, I believe I paid more than adequately for the price of those few cans of gas with my two-year service in the U.S. Army ten years later.

Back in the camp, we wasted no time getting ready for our departure the following morning. As soon as the driver arrived, shortly after sunrise, we loaded our scant belongings on the two-ton truck and a two-wheeled German Army trailer hitched behind it. Then we mounted the truck and climbed on top of the suitcases. How we managed to get everyone—about twenty-five people altogether—on board is still a mystery to me.

As we were about to leave, two ladies with an elderly mother and a teenage daughter rushed toward us and pleaded to join us. Unfortunately, our truck was already overloaded and it was impossible to accept additional people. Finally, we agreed to take the mother and their luggage, leaving the rest of the family to follow us on foot, like most of the fleeing masses. Our destination was Göttingen, a safe haven in the British Zone about eighty miles northwest of Weimar.

Our caravan consisted of the truck, the trailer, and two men who followed us on motorcycles. We started out slowly through the narrow city streets. As we passed a store window, I saw the reflection of our truck in the glass. It was a bizarre sight. We looked like a pack of gypsies huddled on top of their bags. Because of the tall load, the driver had to slow down at every curve in the road to avoid tipping over, and we had to duck each time we passed under trees. Even on a straight highway, we had to curtail our speed because of the massive exodus of people heading west.

The flow of refugees from the east was joined by many Germans who had heard of the Soviet Army's brutalities after the fall of Berlin. They had abandoned their homes and were seeking safety in the western-occupation zones. There were all kinds of people—young and old—on bicycles, motorcycles, and horse-drawn wagons, but the majority were just trudging on foot along the road. Many pushed bicycles or pulled four-wheeled *weggelen* loaded with basic necessities and family heirlooms. I thought how lucky we were to be traveling on the truck. Had we not succeeded in getting gas the night before, we might have been slogging along the dusty road just like the others.

We made a rest stop in a small village where a farmer was selling freshly picked cherries—the first of the season. We bought several liters of those deliciously sweet, luscious berries for munching on the road. I still remember how I savored them and with what gusto I spit the pits overboard. Things were looking up!

After driving a few more miles, we came to an U.S. Army checkpoint. I saw tension in everyone's face. What was wrong? Why had we been stopped? The military policemen asked a few questions, but the driver, who didn't speak English, was unable to answer. Only with Uncle Haakon's intervention were we cleared to continue.

A few minutes later, we arrived at another checkpoint. While Uncle Haakon was talking to the guards, I noticed their strangely shaped helmets that looked like upside-down saucers. Suddenly, it occurred to me that these were the same helmets the British soldiers wore in a World War I movie I had seen in the past. My heart started to race—we were entering the British Zone. Hurrah! We had made it. We were safe at last!

Moments later, Uncle Haakon confirmed the good news and said that we would be going to a temporary refugee center in the city. Teary-eyed from happiness, we started laughing, clapping hands, and singing. We had escaped again.

Whoever would have thought that the flight from the Red Army that started at the Nõmme train station nine months earlier would become an extended marathon with a finish line in Göttingen, guarded by the British Army?

16

Welcome to the British Zone

A S OUR DRIVER was finding his way through the streets of Göttingen, we in the back were relaxed and in high spirits. When we passed the Union Jack, displayed in front of British Army Headquarters, we clapped and cheered. There was no doubt in our minds that we were in the British Zone. Although Göttingen was only a few miles from the border of the realigned Russian Zone, we felt safe and secure under the protection of Her Majesty's Armed Forces.

The local military command had taken over a two-story school building to provide temporary housing for refugees from the east. It sheltered people from many different countries, including some Estonians. The place was a real transit camp—people came and left daily. The living conditions were crowded and not much different from what we'd had in Weimar. There were a few cots for women and children, but the rest of us slept on straw-filled mattresses on the floor. We discovered that our meals came from a British Army kitchen when we were introduced to the new idea of drinking tea and milk together. Soon after our arrival, I met an Estonian boy of my age, Nils. I was glad to have found an Estonian-speaking male friend—the first one since I had come to Germany—for sharing common interests.

We had plenty of free time to explore the historic town of Göttingen, widely known for its centuries-old university, home of many famous scientists and mathematicians. Meandering through the streets, we noticed that it was one of the few cities left untouched by Allied bombings. Years later, I heard that there had been an informal understanding that, as long as the Germans would not bomb Cambridge and Oxford, the Allies would not bomb Göttingen and Heidelberg. That tacit agreement may have saved Göttingen from the agony and destruction that other German cities suffered.

A noticeable contingent of British troops was stationed throughout the city. The soldiers seemed friendly, but more reserved than the affable Americans who showered us with chocolates and candy. The most interesting event was the regular changing-of-the-guard ceremony at army headquarters—a spectacle worth watching. I had never seen a military ceremony like that—the formality, the crisp movements, and foot-stomping were all new to me and to the crowd of curious onlookers. It was the best show in town.

The officer who managed the daily arrival of refugees told Uncle Haakon that an international relief agency, The United Nations Relief and Rehabilitation Administration (UNRRA), operated camps for displaced persons in various locations in British and American Zones. He advised us to move into one of those camps. Since we were already in the British Zone, we decided to remain under the Queen's rule.

We heard many good things about Oldenburg, a city in the northwestern part of Germany. With three DP camps designated for Estonians, it was bound to become a major Estonian center in the British Zone. Therefore, we decided to make it our final destination. Our only problem was getting there. There was no train service, and we couldn't find truck owners interested in driving that far. Finally, Uncle Haakon found someone willing to go as far as Hamelin, about fifty miles north of Göttingen. Better yet, this driver could supply his own gas so that we no longer needed to resort to dubious ways of getting it ourselves. We set the date and started to pack. I had to bid goodbye to Nils, whose family had decided to remain in Göttingen. "I hope to see you again," I said, knowing that the chance of that happening was slim. Little did I know that we would become classmates in Gymnasium three years later.

On the day of our departure, a new problem arose: What to do with the elderly lady to whom we had given a ride from Weimar? Her daughters hadn't shown up yet and we felt uneasy leaving the helpless grandmother alone in a crowd of foreign refugees. Fortunately, our problem was solved when her daughters and granddaughter arrived just hours before our arranged departure time. They were exhausted, sunburned, and leaner than when we had last seen them. They had slogged the whole eighty-mile route together with the fleeing masses we had passed on the road a few days earlier. We were greatly relieved that they had finally arrived and shared the joy of their heartwarming family reunion. When they heard of our travel plans, they immediately wanted to join us. Since some people from our original group had left for other destinations, we had enough room on the truck to accommodate the whole family and its baggage. Everyone seemed pleased as we began the next leg of our journey toward Hamelin.

Hamelin is a small town on Weser River, famous for the folk tale of "The Pied Piper of Hamelin." According to the story, he had used his pipe to rid the town of rats and later to lure away the town's children as well. Life in this sleepy town seemed relatively normal because it had been spared Allied air attacks. All buildings were intact and everything seemed calm and peaceful. We were overjoyed to find accommodations in a hotel. Though it was relatively small, we had comfortable private rooms that even included limited maid service. It was a real luxury after spending weeks in crowded refugee centers. There was also a restaurant next to the hotel. It felt as if the war had completely passed by this town.

What brought us back to reality, however, was the presence of an unusually large number of British troops, particularly military police. The hotel owner told us that the police were there because Nazi war criminals were being held in the town's prison, a place in which Hitler had previously detained political prisoners.

We stayed in Hamelin for almost a week, enjoying every moment of the beautiful summer days. Meanwhile, Uncle Haakon explored various transportation opportunities for the next leg of our journey.

Eventually, he found a truck owner who was willing to take us to Oldenburg, about 130 miles northwest of Hamelin. We were particularly pleased that he, too, could provide his own gas. We packed our bags, climbed onto the truck, and left Hamelin with pleasant memories.

As we embarked on the longest leg of our journey since leaving Weimar, we hoped that it would be the final one for us. We passed a few small towns, scattered among green forests and farmlands, their pretty houses neatly lined up along the roadside. The lilacs were in full bloom, flaunting their lavender and white colors and filling the air with an intoxicating aroma that evoked memories of my summers back home. The weather was good, and everyone was in good humor, relaxing or dozing in the warm sunshine.

The idyllic journey continued until we reached the city limits of Bremen, or for want of a better description, what was left of Bremen. The city had been repeatedly bombed because of its Focke-Wulf fighter aircraft factory and other strategic targets. I had never seen destruction on such a large scale. Everything in sight was leveled to piles of rubble and ash. Occasionally, I could see a broken chimney standing amidst the remains of a burnt-down building. It was the most depressing sight I had ever seen. We drove through endless rows of city blocks, silently staring at the unbelievable devastation. The disturbing images left a deep impression on me. I understood the need to attack military and war-supporting industrial targets, but why would anyone want to destroy an entire city, leaving thousands of people killed, injured, or homeless. After surviving the Jena bombing, I could truly feel the suffering of those unlucky residents of Bremen. I also realized how lucky we had been to survive so many perilous moments of the war. We sat in silence for the remaining part of the trip, trying to come to grips with what we had just seen.

The arrival in Oldenburg awakened us from our gloominess. The city was a pleasant contrast to Bremen. There were no signs of war damage. Trolley buses were running and people were going on with their daily activities. When the driver stopped to get directions to our prospective new home, Camp Bloherfelde, a man on the street asked,

"Are you Estonians?" Our affirmative answer brought a smile to his face.

"So am I. Welcome to Oldenburg," he said and volunteered to guide us to the camp.

As we approached a large *Gasthaus* (country inn), he pointed at it and said, "It's right there." Everybody craned their necks to get a better view.

"What a beautiful place to live," Aunt Senta commented.

Our guide was quick to squash her expectations. "You'll not live in the inn," he said. "It's only a small part of the camp. Most of us live in the wooden barracks behind the inn."

We drove past the *Gasthaus* and pulled up in front of the first barrack. As soon as we had stopped, a small crowd gathered around us.

"Where did you come from?" people kept asking. When they heard that we had started our journey in Weimar, they applauded our timely escape. "You were lucky to get out before the Russians arrived," someone said. "You'll be safe here."

A man stepped forward to greet us. "The first step is registration," he said, "so that we can requisition food for you. Then we have to find a place for you. We've had many new arrivals recently, and we are badly overcrowded. I'm very sorry, but tonight you have to sleep in the storage area until we can find better accommodations."

Another man helped us carry our luggage to our sleeping quarters and gave us army blankets and burlap bags. "You can fill the bags with straw," he said. "We're out of mattresses, but there's plenty of straw in the corner of the room."

As we were stuffing straw into the burlap bags, my mother grumbled, "This is worse than I thought."

"Maybe we should have stayed in Hamelin," Aunt Senta added with a hint of sarcasm.

"Stop whining," admonished Uncle Haakon. "It's only for tonight. Tomorrow we'll get better quarters."

The next morning we lined up early at the front office, hoping to find more decent accommodations. We were shocked and dismayed when we discovered what was meant by "better quarters." Instead of sleeping on the floor in a large storage area with twenty others, we would be sleeping on bunk beds, but still sharing rooms with other families. The camp was, indeed, overcrowded, and the other two camps in the city were in similarly dire condition. My mother and I had to move in with a family of four until better living arrangements could be found.

17

Life in the DP Camp

CAMP BLOHERFELDE was in the outskirts of Oldenburg, conveniently located at the end of the Bloherfelde trolley bus line. It comprised a *Gasthaus* and a cluster of four wooden barracks. The barracks had been previously occupied by the workers of Organisation Todt, the German civil-engineering group responsible for civil and military projects, including the well-known Autobahn highway system. A tiny park separated the drab olive-green barracks from the *Gasthaus*.

The first barrack behind the *Gasthaus* was the main building, which included administrative offices, a clubroom, and the dispensary. The remaining part of the structure was for the residents, who lived in separate rooms on both sides of a long hallway. My mother and I were assigned to share one of those rooms with another family—a doctor, his wife, and their two sons. Although they were not exactly thrilled about the new arrangement, they understood the situation and accepted us graciously. One of the sons, Aavo, was a year older than I and we became friends right away. The room had three bunk beds and a wooden box that served as a small table. The brothers and I were more than happy to sleep on the top bunks, leaving the lower bunks for our parents.

The other barracks had living arrangements similar to ours. Each barrack had common washing and toilet facilities, but no hot water. One of the barracks housed a central kitchen that served hot midday meals. Every day we stood in line and watched the kitchen staff ladle out the "daily special," which we took to eat in our own rooms. Actually, there was nothing special about those meals. Most of the time, we were served plain split-pea soup with a hint of ham. At other times, we received vegetable soup with an occasional piece of meat. On some lucky days we would even find a wiener or macaroni in our bowl. The remaining rations—bread, cheese, and cigarettes—were dispensed from a pantry next to the kitchen. Some people had electric stoves and were able to do light cooking in their own rooms. The food was adequate for survival, but often we had to complement our meager diet with help from the black market.

The most impressive building on the camp site was the Büsselmann's *Gasthaus*, where a group of performing artists lived. Many Estonian actors, singers, and musicians had regrouped in Germany and found their new home in Camp Bloherfelde. They kept their arts alive by entertaining their fellow Estonians in Oldenburg. The *Gasthaus* was ideally suited for them. In addition to their living quarters, it had a large multipurpose room with a stage that was used for theater and concert performances, dances, and other large gatherings. During the day, it was mostly used for playing volleyball and basketball. Occasionally, a group of Canadian officers reserved it for badminton. Every time they played, a small group of men gathered by the entrance and waited for the game to end so that they could rush in and scavenge for cigarette butts. Good American tobacco was in high demand, and the smokers really didn't care where it came from.

In addition to Camp Bloherfelde, there were two other DP camps for Estonians in Oldenburg: Camp Sandplatz and Camp Ohmstede. The latter was the largest camp to provide shelter for refugees from Latvia and Lithuania as well. Altogether, there were close to 1200 Estonians living in the three camps. All camps were directly under local British military command, while funding and supplies came from the refugee relief organization UNRRA. The military officer in charge of our camp was a convivial Australian Army major. He understood why we couldn't return to our homeland and tried to help us whenever possible. Although the British Army was in charge, the camps were actually self-governed—each camp had its own administration for managing daily operations.

Reverend Stockholm, with whom we had shared the air-raid shelter in Jena, was our camp's Commandant. Soon after our arrival, he asked Uncle Haakon to manage the daily operations of the camp as Assistant Commandant. My mother's fluency in English and German, along with her recently acquired typing skills, qualified her for a position as the camp's secretary. In addition to normal secretarial duties, she had to report daily the number of people in camp in order for residents to receive the proper amount of food and cigarette rations. It was a challenging task because the camp's population fluctuated, changing almost daily in the early months. Her secret to having adequate food supplies for everyone at all times was that she posted all newcomers promptly while being a bit tardy when it came to reporting departing residents.

There were numerous paid positions in the camp: police, doctors, nurses, kitchen workers, and maintenance people. Their salary in German reichsmarks was insignificant compared to the value of the extra cigarette rations they received. As a working woman, my mother received six packs of American cigarettes per month; male workers received twice as many. The highest cigarette rations—18 packs—went to the camp's policemen because their work was deemed the most stressful. Non-workers were entitled to only one pack of cigarettes per month. Several men worked off-camp directly for UNRRA, mostly as automobile or truck drivers. Those were highly coveted jobs because, in addition to a regular salary, they provided generous cigarette rations and brand-new navy-blue military uniforms.

Because of my mother's position, we were able to get better accommodations—a room to share with Uncle Karli and Aunt Olli. We were delighted to be together with them, not to mention the added space and privacy that we gained. The doctor, with whom we had shared a room previously, became the official camp doctor and therefore was entitled to keep that room exclusively for his family.

What we needed most urgently, however, was hot water. Since Estonians enjoy saunas as passionately as Finns do, we had to have a real sauna. UNRRA provided the necessary building material, and with the effort of many enthusiastic volunteers, the sauna was completed within a week or two.

I still remember the celebrated opening day. Nearly everybody showed up for a long-awaited opportunity to bathe with hot water and to enjoy the pleasures of a traditional Estonian sauna. It was sheer delight to sit in the cloud of steam arising from the hot rocks and to beat myself gently with a bunch of fragrant birch branches. When the heat became unbearable, I stepped out for a quenching with cold water, only to return to the steam room for more enjoyment (or punishment, depending on one's opinion). It brought back pleasant memories of my summers on Uncle Karli's farm, where sauna was a Saturday afternoon ritual.

Another urgent project was the construction of an additional barrack to alleviate the overcrowding. Building materials were again furnished by UNRRA, and the work of assembling the prefabricated components was accomplished by volunteers. The walls were easy to assemble, but barely adequate for protection against outside elements in the winter. The inside walls did offer some privacy, but you were out of luck if your neighbors happened to be of the noisy or nosy kind. This new barrack became the most desirable building in the camp because it was equipped with central heating. It also had a limited number of small rooms for two- and three-member families. My mother and I were elated to get one of those small rooms, which we shared with Grandmother. We had more privacy, and Grandmother helped us with many household chores while my mother was working in the office

As soon as we had settled in, my mother decided to let Aunt Iti in Tallinn know that we had successfully managed to escape and were safe and living in West Germany. Sending a letter directly to her would have been unwise. We still remembered how Soviet secret agents had confiscated all of our foreign correspondence. A letter from a close relative in West Germany could have had serious consequences for the recipient. To avoid causing potential harm to anyone, my mother sent an open postcard, addressed to the pharmacy, with a cryptic message that we were alive and well. She hoped that someone would understand the message and pass it on to Aunt Iti.

Although we felt secure living in the British Zone, we were still uncertain about our future. The Soviet Union had gained significant control over most of Eastern Europe and was aggressively campaigning to repatriate all refugees to their home countries. There were rumors that we, too, might be forced to return to occupied Estonia. Fortunately, the Americans and the British opposed sending us home against our will, but they did agree to let communist representatives visit the camps and present their case for our return.

Our camp did not escape such a visit. Without much notice, a communist representative, accompanied by a British officer, arrived to lure us with his propaganda speech. Although no one had any intention of returning, we went to hear him out of curiosity. The speaker was a short man who spoke fluent Estonian with a slight Russian accent. Everyone listened in silence. He said that life in the "Estonian Soviet Republic" was returning to normal after the war and we would have nothing to fear upon returning—no one would be persecuted. As he extolled the "virtues" of returning to our homeland, a young boy with an axe in his hand walked in, apparently looking for his father. Unable to find him, he turned his attention to the speaker and gave him a serious, almost menacing, look. The audience saw it as a symbolic message that the speaker was unwelcome and gave the boy loud applause. The startled speaker looked puzzled and tried to continue, but to no avail. He had lost the audience. People began to talk and walked out of the meeting. No one accepted his invitation.

Yet, we still carried a hope in our hearts of returning to Estonia, wishing that it would once again be a free country. Many times late at night, I fantasized about going there as a member of the American Army and liberating Tallinn from Soviet occupation. I would be standing in a jeep, driving though jubilant crowds holding flowers, like the Parisians who had welcomed the Americans when they liberated Paris. But as time went on, I began to realize that it was just a pipe dream and that I should get used to living in the camp.

Life in the camp was a totally new experience for me. Despite the poor living conditions, I found it interesting and exciting. There were a lot of young people of my age and many opportunities for organized sports and social activities. It was a refreshing change from the unsettled times I'd experienced since leaving Estonia. My mother, on the other hand, didn't share my enthusiasm. She found the crowded living conditions, lack of privacy, and poor food difficult to accept.

We did have some happy moments on the days when CARE packages arrived from America and we rushed to claim our share. Those days reminded me of Christmas because everyone acted like a child finding presents under a Christmas tree. I remember the sheer excitement of opening a package and discovering various surprises inside: New Zealand mutton, canned beans, milk powder, cheese, chocolate bars, cookies, and other goodies. Occasionally, we would find a can of real coffee—a true treat for coffee lovers, or a precious bartering item for others.

Fresh eggs were always in short supply. The shortage became particularly acute at Easter. Every family wanted to have a few colored eggs for the traditional egg-knocking. A couple of UNRRA drivers decided to solve the problem by driving to the country on Easter weekend. They would buy eggs by the dozens from local farmers and sell them individually at the camp for a nice profit. However, on the way back, their Volkswagen bug went off the road, crushing the precious cargo, and damaging the front fender. The fact that the drivers had celebrated their successful purchase with a few shots of schnapps probably had something to do with the unfortunate accident. I still remember the embarrassed faces of the drivers as they tried to explain to the families what had happened and why they now had to celebrate Easter without eggs. For drivers, the loss of the eggs was no less painful than having to clean the inside of the car and repair the dented fender in front of curious kibitzers, who offered more advice than was necessary. By working around the clock all through the holiday, they were able to finish the repair and return the car to the motor pool as if nothing had happened. They were lucky to keep their jobs and, most importantly, their generous cigarette rations.

We could also buy some food from the camp store, but the store was small and the entrepreneur who operated it charged black-market prices for whatever merchandise he happened to have at hand. But almost always he had two barrels in the corner of the store: one for salty herring, the other for pickled cucumbers.

If we couldn't find what we wanted in the store, we could also look for it on the bulletin board. In addition to official announcements, people posted various types of personal messages. Someone might be searching for a relative lost in the war; another would offer something for sale. The best attention-getting ads were simple and pictorial. An ad for eggs would have a sketch of an egg with the room number of the seller in the bottom corner. Other goods like fish, sausages, and mushrooms were promoted in a similar way. It was an effective way to overcome language barriers in the ethnically mixed camps. It also worked well in our camp, until a mysterious ad appeared, featuring a sketch of a partially naked woman and next to it the room number of two girls who were known to have late-night parties. The girls were enraged by the suggestive ad and demanded justice. I believe they received an apology from the front office, but the anonymous trickster was never found, leaving the gossipers plenty to gab about.

Not only was food scarce, so was everything else in post-war Germany. Electricity was rationed by rolling blackouts, where sections of the city had the power turned off an hour at a time. Because candles were scarce, we spent blackout periods mostly in darkness, either sleeping or enjoying conversations in the dark. A friend of mine, an avid reader, came up with a clever idea for coping with the blackout. At the start of the blackout, he selected a book for reading and boarded a well-lighted electric trolley bus in front of the *Gasthaus* and rode it to the end of the line and back, just in time for lights to come back on at the camp.

We also had local blackouts caused by excessive use of electricity. Many people used electric hotplates for heating their rooms, which caused circuit breakers to overload, particularly on cold winter days. I remember the barrack warden walking up and down the hallway, warning everybody in his bellowing voice to turn off their electric appliances. But many were reluctant to heed his advice, assuming that it applied to their neighbors, but not to them. The result was that the circuit breakers became overloaded and the whole building was thrown into darkness.

Lack of adequate clothing was also a serious problem. The clothing we'd brought from Estonia was wearing out and I was outgrowing mine. The British Army provided regular army jackets, dyed in different colors for civilian use. Mine was brown and I wore it to school and around the camp most of the time. Grandmother, who had bought a used sewing machine, made me a pair of pants from a German Army blanket to go with the jacket. For special occasions, I wore the discarded German Air Force uniform we had found in Bergern. Once in a while, we received shipments of clothing from American charities. The items were distributed on a lottery basis. I was lucky to draw a low number in two different lotteries and became the proud owner of a pair of black leather shoes and a well-fitting sport coat.

All boys of my age were overjoyed when a shipment of sporting goods arrived with brand new American-made sneakers, called Keds. We wore them every day, proudly showing them off, just like American kids parade their Nike shoes today.

Occasionally, door-to-door salesmen would come by with their suitcases to peddle whatever trinkets they had for sale. Grandmother could never say no to them. She invited them in and made them empty their suitcases on her bed and explain every detail about each item. She asked many questions and haggled over prices, but seldom bought anything. She enjoyed the whole process, though I hated the chaos it caused. But there was nothing I could do about it—Grandmother was Grandmother.

For most purchases, people paid with cigarettes or bartered. American cigarettes were the most valuable item and regarded as "real money." A pack was considered the equivalent of 100 reichs-marks. A cigarette slipped to the cashier at a movie box office always got you a good seat. To illustrate the enormous purchasing power of American cigarettes, I recall the time when I accidentally chipped my two front teeth during field practice. The repair required major dental work—gold fillings with ceramic overlays. It took several visits to a German dentist, who spent hours to complete his work and make me look presentable again. The charge for his magnificent work was 200 reichsmarks, the price of two packs of cigarettes! Of course, I had to provide my own gold, which came from Grandmother, who had a gold bridge she no longer needed. For ten more cigarettes, the dentist filled a cavity as well.

I couldn't wait for my sixteenth birthday because then I would be officially recognized as a grownup and become eligible for cigarette rations. Though it was only one pack per month, it was the best birth-day gift I could have wished for. Because cigarettes were too valuable for smoking, I saved mine and used them sparingly only to buy things I needed. I still remember the day when our scheduled allotment of cigarettes didn't arrive on time and we received chewing tobacco in-stead. My friends and I had never seen chewing tobacco and we won-dered what to do with it. Considering that it wouldn't be worth much on the black market, we decided to try it ourselves. We removed the wrapping and chewed that brown stuff as if it were chewing gum. A little while later, I felt nauseous and had to rush to the toilet. As I was dropping my breakfast in the toilet, my friends arrived, one by one, pale as ghosts, and did the same. No one had bothered to tell us that chewing tobacco was different from chewing gum, that instead of swallowing the juice, we were supposed to spit it out.

Because of the high price of cigarettes, many smokers switched to pipes. Uncle Karli, an avid pipe smoker from his days in Estonia, was always looking for new sources of pipe tobacco. One day he hap-pened to meet a German woman who worked in a local cigarette factory. She offered him tobacco that had been rejected from the pro-duction line for being too coarse for cigarettes, but was perfectly good for smoking in a pipe. Recognizing a great business opportunity,

Uncle Karli accepted her offer. He bought tobacco from her in bulk and resold it in small quantities to other pipe smokers in the camp. Before long, he had an ongoing business with a growing number of regular customers.

18

Going Back to School

PERHAPS THE MOST significant achievement of the DP camps was the swift launching of Estonian-language schools for the countless youths whose education had been interrupted by the war. The Oldenburg Estonian Gymnasium opened its doors in the fall of 1945, and I was among the first to enroll. We shared classrooms with a German school that was within walking distance from Camp Bloherfelde. The students came from all three DP camps and included a few who lived independently in the city. I was delighted to see such a large gathering of Estonian-speaking teenagers and to be back in a classroom after what seemed a long year of absence.

The majority of teachers were experienced professionals who had previously taught in Estonia and seemed as happy as we were to be back in the classroom. Because we didn't have Estonian-language textbooks, they had spent hours preparing handwritten course notes, which we copied painstakingly during class. Some of the teachers even bought school supplies with their own money, often at black-market prices.

We also had a few teachers who were new to pedagogy. Although they lacked teaching experience, they were experts in their subject areas. One such person was my math teacher, Jaan Raud. His academic degree from Tartu University was actually in agriculture, but he knew and loved mathematics and was excellent at explaining it.

Dark-haired and brown-eyed, he didn't look like a typical Estonian. There was something about him that was special. With his penetrating eyes and commanding voice he captured everyone's undivided attention. He made the principles of algebra so simple that almost everyone was able to grasp them. And when it came to geometry, he made it easy for us to visualize the shapes and sizes of various objects and understand their relationships.

Mr. Raud had a unique method exceptionally well suited for teaching mathematics and science under our constrained circumstances. Since we didn't have textbooks, we came to each class without prior knowledge of the topic for the day. Mr. Raud began every class by introducing a new problem for which each of us had to develop a solution, usually in the form of an equation or a formula. After he had finished explaining the assignment, he left us alone to scratch our heads and ponder in silence. As soon as a student had figured out a solution, he was to raise his hand. Mr. Raud would then walk quietly to the student, examine the answer, and either approve it or give hints for further reflection. He repeated this process until half of the class had successfully arrived at the solution. Then he rearranged the seating of the entire class. Students who had solved the problem moved next to the ones who hadn't and helped them. Finally, Mr. Raud walked to the blackboard, showed us step-by-step how to develop a general formula, and explained its application to real-world problems.

I couldn't imagine a better way to learn something new than struggling on one's own, feeling the exhilaration of an "aha" moment, and mastering that knowledge well enough to teach others. This method, where the teacher acted as a coach rather than a lecturer, clearly seemed superior to the traditional one of presenting a solution for students to memorize without gaining true understanding of the subject.

For years, I wondered whether some form of this method would be of value in other schools, until I learned of the successful adoption of "discovery learning" in Japanese schools and of a growing interest in similar methods in American schools. I believe that Jaan Raud, a man with no pedagogical background, was a true pioneer in the field of education.

Mr. Raud had a full arsenal of various ways to stimulate our minds. At the end of a class, he would often challenge us to come up with quick verbal answers to simple arithmetic problems. He also taught us useful shortcuts and clever tricks for solving problems and remembering arithmetic equations. Whenever we got ahead of schedule, he kept us amused with puzzles and clever jokes.

He was demanding, but he was also fair. He insisted on discipline, respect, and proper behavior in the classroom. When we wanted to say something, we had to raise our hands, and stand up, and the boys had to have their jackets buttoned up. If you hadn't done your homework and told him about it before the class, he accepted this as an honest admission and didn't hold it against you. But any student who tried to deceive him was in for serious trouble.

Cheating was absolutely unacceptable in his class. Several students learned this the hard way during the first quiz. He gave us a problem to solve and warned us not to cheat. He then proceeded to wander through the classroom, admiring the photographs on the wall. A few students took advantage of his apparent interest in the photos and couldn't resist the temptation to peek over a classmate's shoulder. None of us noticed that the glass under which the photos had been framed acted as a mirror, giving him full view of the classroom.

Suddenly, he turned around and announced, "Some of you have been cheating." Then he called out the names of the guilty ones and said to them, "Turn in your papers and leave the classroom. You failed the quiz." We were stunned, frozen in our seats. The uneasy silence was broken only by a girl's hushed sobbing. "Don't you ever try to cheat in my class," he said. "You won't be able to get away with it. I remember every trick there is from my own student days."

From that day on, no one cheated in his class. There was only one boy who tried, and he was caught. To make things worse, he lied in his attempt to cover it up. The whole class could see the fury in Mr. Raud's eyes. "You committed a major offense in my class," he bellowed. "You are banned from all social activities in the camp for two weeks. I don't want to see your face in the *Gasthaus*, clubroom, or out on the sports field."

A week later, there was some kind of a celebration in the *Gasthaus* with music and dancing. Almost everyone in the camp was there, except the banned boy, who was outside standing behind a window, longingly watching the festivities inside. When Jaan Raud noticed him, he went out and invited him in. "You can come in now," he said. "You have suffered enough already. I hope you learned your lesson."

Although Mr. Raud demanded respect and discipline in the classroom, he treated us as his equals outside the school. Since we all lived in close quarters, I saw him often—standing in the food line, perspiring in the sauna, or chopping firewood behind the barracks. It was always fun to be in his company. He was a superb father figure for me and several other boys who had lost their fathers during the Soviet occupation.

If any boy needed help with homework, we could always attend Mr. Raud's boiler-room sessions. Those took place whenever he was on boiler-room duty (all men in our barrack had to take turns keeping an eye on the wood-burning boiler for central heating). There he helped us understand some of the finer points we may have missed in the classroom and entertained questions on a variety of other subjects. In return, he expected us to help him bring in firewood and pile it up along the wall. I also attended those sessions, not because I needed tutoring, but for the fun of being in his company. Besides, the boiler room was the warmest place to be on frigid winter days.

When three of my classmates and I wanted to skip a grade in school, Jaan Raud volunteered to tutor us during the summer recess. Every weekday morning we spent a couple of hours with him in the camp's conference room. Those were some of the most stimulating hours that I can recall. Invigorated by a cool morning breeze, we sat around a table and brainstormed the challenging problems he gave us. He was a master in motivating and stimulating our brains to a level we hadn't experienced before. Unfortunately, those happy sessions came to an end when he left for Canada during the first emigration wave in 1947. We abandoned our plans and stayed in our regular class.

My second-year class in Oldenburg Estonian Gymnasium.
Mr. Raud is in the front row, center

Shortly before Mr. Raud left, he went with a few students to visit a sick classmate at a hospital. Huddled around the hospital bed, we had a candid discussion about school and our teachers. One boy perfectly captured our shared sentiment when he looked at Jaan Raud and said, "At first, when you started teaching us, we thought you were the biggest son of a bitch in the world. But as time went by, we learned to appreciate you for the kind person you really are and how much you have done for us. We are truly grateful for that. We will miss you."

Perhaps I am the most grateful of his students. Jaan Raud was the best teacher I ever had. After my father was arrested, I had trouble concentrating and lost interest in schoolwork. Though I still managed to get decent grades, my passion for learning was gone. Jaan Raud was able to motivate me and restore that passion. He managed to renew my interest in mathematics, which became the foundation for my career in engineering. He taught us not only mathematics, but how to become mature and responsible citizens as well. Aside from my parents, he was the most influential person in my life.

My classmates were truly fortunate to have Jaan Raud's leadership and guidance at an age when we most needed it. He was there by sheer stroke of luck, having survived a tragedy at sea while fleeing from the Russians. He and his wife, who was pregnant at the time, were on board the *Moero*, the hospital ship that was torpedoed and sunk by Soviet bombers in the Baltic Sea. They were among the few survivors who were rescued after floating in frigid waters for hours. They lost all their belongings, but worst of all, Mrs. Raud lost their unborn baby shortly afterward. However, they did not dwell on their tragedy as some others did, but moved on to start a new life with a positive outlook that was so contagious it helped many of his students achieve more than we ever considered possible.

We had two other math teachers after Jaan Raud. Although neither one of them had taught mathematics before, they were good teachers who made the subject relevant to us. I was struck by the way they taught the practical importance of mathematics, each explaining it from his own professional perspective. For example, Major Võhma, a former artillery officer who taught trigonometry, stressed the importance of speed. "When you are on the battlefield," he said, "you need to calculate the enemy's position, point the gun, and fire it faster than he can do it. Otherwise you'll be dead."

On the other hand, Mr. Liefländer, a civil engineer who taught analytic geometry and calculus, saw the world differently. "Take your time," he said. "Check and double-check all your calculations. If a bridge collapses because of an error in your calculations, you'll lose both your job and reputation. In some countries you may even end up in jail."

Overall, we had a rich and varied curriculum. We were required to study many subjects, including Latin, German, English and Estonian languages, chemistry, physics, religion, philosophy, geography, economics, natural sciences, drawing, and music.

Although I did well in most subjects, I found history the least inspiring. We spent an enormous amount of time studying ancient Greek and Roman history, where the focus was on memorizing the birth and death dates of kings and emperors. I never found out why they fought each other or why some societies flourished and others perished. Despite that, I was able to pass with intensive cramming a few days before the exam.

In chemistry class we suffered from a lack of laboratory facilities. We memorized by rote the Periodic Table and basic principles of chemistry without the benefit of hands-on experimentation. The teacher performed a few experiments in front of the class, using his daughter's play dishes, but no matter how hard he tried, he couldn't get me to share his excitement about chemistry. It was not a good start for a boy who was supposed to become a pharmacist.

Nor did I have much enthusiasm for Latin. I learned as much as necessary to understand Latin phrases like "*Carpe diem*" and "*Sic transit gloria mundi*," but not enough to master the finer points of the language. Although the teacher, Reverend Nuudi, who also taught religion, was an outstanding instructor and a good storyteller, he still couldn't arouse my interest for a language that I considered archaic. I wish he had been my history teacher.

I was more interested in learning English because of its wide-spread use throughout the world. It was taught by Mr. Rippe, a well-qualified, Oxford-educated German. He couldn't get a teaching job in the German schools because school officials were suspicious of his activities in England during the war. As a result, he found a niche teaching English in the Estonian Gymnasium and giving private lessons on the side. My mother even took a few lessons with him to brush up on her English.

The capstone reading in the final year was Charles Dickens's *A Christmas Carol*. It had been standard reading for the graduating class in Estonia, and therefore, we too were subjected to studying Ebenezer Scrooge's ethical transformation. I remember struggling with Dickens's vocabulary, and I hated the tedious chore of looking up words that I never expected to use again. I preferred reading modern British and American literature, which I did on my own during summer recess. I remember reading an American novel where the word "guy" was used rather frequently. My unsuccessful attempts to find the meaning of that baffling word led to days of frustration because I couldn't find in my English dictionary. Mr. Rippe was away on summer vacation, and no one whom I asked knew the answer. Finally, I concluded that all men in America are called guys.

In Estonian class we spent hours and hours mastering the grammar of what is considered one of the most complex of European languages. Fortunately, the pronouns in Estonian don't have gender, so we didn't have to worry about being politically correct. In the more advanced classes we studied not only Estonian classics, but were also exposed to some important English and American authors as well. The word "nevermore" still rings in my ears every time someone brings up the name Edgar Allan Poe.

Music classes were only for those who had musical talent or at least showed some potential. When the teacher heard my off-key rendition of "You are My Sunshine," she cringed and promptly exempted me from her class.

The school offered no formal physical education or sports program. It really wasn't necessary because each camp had its own organized sports teams, and we played frequently against each other. I recall only one time in my final year when we formed volleyball and basketball teams of our students to play against the Estonian Gymnasium in Lingen, another major Estonian DP center near the Dutch border. We selected the best players to represent our school and left for Lingen to find out who would be the champions. It was a memorable trip. Traveling in the back of a small military truck, we were full of energy and enthusiasm. As we passed through the gates of the Lingen camp, we sang the words of an old Estonian fighting song at the top of our lungs: "We will return victorious or we will fall." The fact that Lingen Gymnasium was bigger and had superior teams didn't dampen our spirit. Our ace was a young Estonian volleyball star, my friend Nils from my days in Göttingen, who had played at the mere age of sixteen on the Estonian national team against the American All Star team on its European tour. On the first day of the competition we played volleyball, and we lost. Unfortunately, we also lost in basketball the following day. Regardless of the losses, we had a wonderful time, made new friends, and danced with the Lingen girls until the early morning hours.

After the first two years, we had to leave our original school building and move into the barracks at Camp Ohmstede. These new classrooms were deplorable. I hated the poor lighting and acoustics, not to mention the rickety tables and chairs. I had to get up early and commute by trolley to the other end of the city. It was particularly hard during the winter, when the boys took turns coming to school ahead of the other students, to light the wood-burning furnaces and warm up the classrooms before the day's instruction started. Despite our most diligent efforts, those classrooms remained uncomfortably chilly most of the time.

After less than a year of dreadful conditions in Camp Ohmstede, we moved to a more centrally located former church school next to Camp Sandplatz. The classrooms were much better there, but still far from ideal. It was not until my final year that we moved into a magnificent German Gymnasium building near midtown. It had the best facilities, and its central location made it convenient for students from all three camps.

My last-year class of Oldenburg Estonian Gymnasium. Reverend Nuudi is in the front row, center

Despite many difficult conditions, the quality of our education was surprisingly high. Out of my graduating class of fourteen, almost everyone went to college. One boy pursued a military career, and two girls preferred the title of "Mrs." Most of us emigrated to the United States, a few went to Canada, and one remained in Germany. Of those who went to college, all graduated, and seven continued to earn advanced degrees: four Master's degrees, and three doctorates. Those remarkable achievements are a tribute to our teachers, whose unselfish dedication and hard work made such accomplishments possible. Years later, in the United States, I had the opportunity of meeting several of them again, including Jaan Raud and his lovely wife, and to express my personal gratitude. I wish I could have met all of them to say, "Thank you for opening the door to our future."

19

Sports, Culture, and Entertainment

THERE WAS NEVER a dull moment in the camp, not for a teenage boy like me. Besides school and homework, there were many athletic activities to choose from. We had no shortage of older athletes willing to teach and train us in all types of sports. Volleyball was the most popular team sport; it became my favorite as well. We played outdoors in the summer and moved into the *Gasthaus* when the weather turned cold and wet in the fall. I also tried my hand at basketball, but discovered early on that I didn't have adequate stamina to become a serious player. I was just as happy to practice dribbling and taking occasional shots at the basket.

There were many organized track-and-field events for us to determine who was the fastest runner or who could leap farther or jump higher than others. We could also try our hand at shot-put, javelin, and discus. I managed to do well in the broad jump and triple jump, probably because of the slight advantage from my big feet and lightweight body. I never had any interest in boxing, but when we received several pairs of boxing gloves, I had to give it a try. Without any training, and at my buddies' urging, I entered an improvised ring to face my classmate, Heino, who was about my size and weight. The match didn't last long; I ran out of breath and Heino had a bloody nose. That was the end of my boxing career.

My true passion was ping-pong, called table tennis by serious players. The game room was only steps away from our room, and I was always there at the first sound of the bouncing ball. Like every-thing else at the time, balls were in short supply. When they began to crack from vigorous playing, we repaired them with nail polish or bought new ones on the black market. The long hours spent at the ping-pong table paid off when I became the junior champion at Camp Bloherfelde, which qualified me to play in the Baltic tournament against Latvians and Lithuanians.

My first game was against a seasoned Latvian opponent who played an excellent defensive game. With carefully placed curve shots, he tempted me to slam more frequently than I should have. I lost the game and the opportunity to play in the next round. I was shocked and disappointed, but it was a great experience that brought my inflated ego back to earth.

The Boy Scouts and Girl Scouts of Camp Bloherfelde

A good part of my time was spent on Boy Scouts activities. Each camp had its Boy Scout and Girl Scout unit. I joined the one in Camp Bloherfelde as soon it was organized. Under the leadership of two charismatic and dedicated scoutmasters, we spent many hours learning a variety of useful skills. We played the Kim's Game to strengthen our capacity to observe and remember details; we learned

Morse code, and how to use a compass for finding our way through open fields and forests. But the best part of scouting was summer camp, where we could put all those skills to practice in the woods. The evenings by the campfire where we sang and told stories were particularly enjoyable, leaving fond memories for many years. The Boy Scout's motto "Be Prepared" and the slogan "Do a Good Turn Daily" are principles that have served me well throughout my life.

By the time I turned sixteen, my interests shifted toward the YMCA, which offered activities more appropriate for my age. A two-week YMCA-sponsored summer camp was particularly exciting and memorable. The camp was not far from the city, but far enough to be out in the wild. The dirt road to the camp led to a small building next to three flagpoles on which the flags of the Baltic countries flew, signifying that the boys came from Estonia, Latvia, and Lithuania. The building contained an open-air kitchen, where the cooks served far better meals than we had back at the home camp. We got to enjoy the kind of nourishing meals that our growing bodies craved: oatmeal and scrambled eggs for breakfast; wieners or meatballs for dinner. Though the scrambled eggs were made from egg powder and mashed potatoes were whipped from potato flakes, we devoured every serving and went back to the line for seconds.

The downhill path toward the river led to volleyball and basketball courts on the left and a cluster of tents under pine trees on the right. Working together with my three friends, we pitched our tent and decorated it with stones, twigs, and moss to give it a unique character.

The days were filled with sports and games, the evenings with camaraderie and singing around the campfire. When it came to sports, we were extremely competitive. The Lithuanians dominated in basketball, but in volleyball the Estonians were in a fierce competition with the Latvians. The final game was so evenly matched that we were thoroughly exhausted when we finished with a narrow victory. It was a memorable game. The following day we had closing ceremonies where we lowered the flags, and then everyone returned to their home camps.

To keep the DPs entertained in the camp, there was a movie night each week. The room was always crowded despite the small screen, poor sound quality, and a dreadful choice of films. Most of the time we were shown American western movies of Hopalong Cassidy's adventures, which always ended with the killing of the bad guys. At the end of one show, I heard someone grumble, "This wasn't as good as the last week's movie—only five men were killed."

For something better than western films, we had to go to the movie theaters in town, where the latest German, American, and British films were shown. The most popular movie at the time was *Die Frau Meiner Träume* (*The Woman of my Dreams*), with the popular film star Marika Rökk. It was restricted for anyone under eighteen. Being only sixteen, obviously it became a must-see movie for me and my underaged friends. I was lucky to get into the theater and see it at my first attempt. It was a great movie, somewhat in the style of 1930s Hollywood musicals—all in full color. I was mesmerized by the superb singing and dancing. The whole film was in good taste, with no risqué scenes, leaving me wondering why it was considered inappropriate for teenagers. I liked it so much that I went to see it again with some older friends of mine. But this time I was challenged by a stern policewoman who insisted on seeing formal proof of my age. As my older friends were let into the theater, I was left standing on the street, deeply embarrassed and disappointed. My only consolation was that I already had seen it.

Back at the camp, dancing was popular on Saturday nights. I still remember how I learned to dance during my first year in camp at the age of fourteen. I was standing with a few other boys at the clubroom door, listening to the music and watching the dancers. None of us knew how to dance. The camp kindergarten teacher, a young woman with stunning blonde hair, noticed us and decided to introduce us to the world of dancing. She came over with open arms and asked, "Would anyone like to dance with me?"

My friends vanished at lightning speed, leaving me behind as her only victim. I had no choice but to accept her invitation. As we stepped onto the dance floor, she whispered to me, "Don't worry. Just do like the others do."

It was an old-fashioned dance, called *vengerka*, which didn't require much grace or skill. Once I had overcome my initial fear of dancing in front of other people, I actually began to enjoy it. "You did fine," my partner said, "but for more modern dances, you'll need some lessons. I'll talk to your friends and see if they might be interested." I was surprised at how fast she managed to convince a small group of teenage boys and girls that ballroom dancing was an important social skill we had to learn, and that she was the right person to teach us. After we had learned the basic steps of the waltz and foxtrot, we began looking for opportunities to put our newly learned skills into practice.

First, we had to find someone to provide music for our group. We decided that Mr. Pärn would be just the right person. An easygoing tall man with a mustache and curly hair, he was a gifted accordionist whose wide repertoire of popular music was ideal for dancing. Since I lived in the same barrack with him, I agreed to talk to him. I knocked on his door and said, "Mister Pärn, there are a lot of young people who would like to dance tonight. Would you please play for us?"

"Sure. But do you have enough people?" he asked.

"Yes, we do. Please come!"

"If you say so, then I'll come." He slung his accordion over his shoulder and we walked to the clubroom. The room was empty. Mr. Pärn looked annoyed. "There is no one here. I am not going to play for an empty room," he grumbled and walked away. I ran to round up my friends, who had been reluctant to come until we had music. Finally, after a few trips back and forth, I was able to convince Mr. Pärn that people were, indeed, ready and waiting for his grand entrance.

This chicken-and-egg routine took place almost every time we wanted to dance. But once the dances had begun, they became a success not only for us youngsters, but for all who loved to dance— young and old. When people heard the music, they came to listen and then joined the dancers on the floor. Even my math teacher, Jaan Raud, came with his lovely wife. They were a wonderful pair to watch on the dance floor. Whether it was a waltz or a tango, they glided as gracefully as Fred Astaire and Ginger Rogers in the movies. Sometimes they would show my friends and me how to look less awkward on the floor, and they even taught us some new steps.

As time went by, the dances became routine Saturday-night events and my organizing help was no longer needed. A newly formed band, composed of a piano, accordion, trumpet, guitar, and drums, replaced Mr. Pärn's accordion music. Dancing was a newly discovered pleasure, since public dancing had been prohibited under Nazi rule during the war. Initially, our music and dances were from the pre-war years, but it didn't take us long to discover British and American music.

The British introduced the "Hokey Pokey" craze, which quickly captured everybody's imagination. It was a simple dance as the words suggested:

"You put your right foot in, you put your right foot out,
You put your right foot in, and you shake it all about,
You do the hokey pokey and you turn yourself around,
That what it's all about."

Next you extended your left foot, then the right and left arms, and then, as the dance progressed, you moved on to more interesting body parts. Once a couple of British officers had demonstrated the basic steps, a few other couples followed their example and soon almost everyone was on the dance floor. It was hilarious to see elderly men with horn-rimmed glasses and prim and proper ladies lose their inhibitions and wiggle their buttocks in wild gyrations. Forgetting the drabness of everyday life, they enjoyed their few moments of frivolity.

The "Hokey Pokey" craze didn't last very long. It lost its popularity when American popular music began to spread throughout West Germany. It reached the camps in the British Zone more slowly than in the American sector because we didn't have direct contact with the Americans, nor did we own many radios at that time. Therefore, it was a major event when two young Estonian accordionists from the

American Zone came to perform the latest American tunes to a jam-packed crowd in the *Gasthaus*. Everyone fell in love with songs like "Sentimental Journey" and "Besame Mucho," but the typically reserved Estonians became ecstatic when they heard the rhythmic beat of "In the Mood." It was not exactly the Glenn Miller arrangement, but the dual-accordion rendition was exciting enough to set the crowd on fire and demand encores.

Almost every Estonian camp had a folk-dancing group for the purpose of keeping a national tradition alive. When a couple of enthusiasts invited me to join their dance group, I couldn't say no. The group consisted of six couples. I was fortunate to find a talented and graceful dance partner, named Monika, who had a natural gift for dancing. Although she lived in Camp Ohmstede, she commuted faithfully by trolley to our camp several times a week. After weeks of practice and rehearsals, we were ready to step on stage, dressed in our colorful traditional costumes. In the beginning, we performed for people in our own camp, but later we entertained other audiences, including the local British Army units.

Folk dancing in the park

We were particularly fortunate to have several accomplished performing artists living in Camp Bloherfelde. Two stars from the former

Estonian Opera, Helmi Aaren and Maret Pank, performed on countless occasions for appreciative audiences in the *Gasthaus* hall. They were usually accompanied by the classical concert pianist Dagmar Kokker, who had already received wide acclaim for her solo performances back in Estonia. The musicians toured other DP camps in both the British and American Zones and also delighted German audiences from Hamburg to Bayreuth.

The soloists were not the only performers to attract attention beyond the camp's borders. Choral music had been deeply embedded in Estonian culture, as epitomized by song festivals where local choruses came together from all parts of the country to express their love for the music, and for the country. To keep that tradition alive, almost every Estonian DP camp had some form of a choral group. Two such groups in Oldenburg were the Estonian Male Chorus and a mixed chorus. The male chorus, with a repertoire ranging from traditional Estonian songs to the music of Puccini and Verdi, received accolades in many DP camps as well as in major German concert halls.

With the presence of so many performing artists in Oldenburg, the city became the major Estonian cultural center in the British Zone. The umbrella organization was the Estonian National Theater, which had over thirty performers and support staff. It offered about a dozen productions—mostly by Estonian playwrights—over a three-year time period. Of all the performances I attended, the most memorable one was the Estonian-language production of Tennessee Williams' *The Glass Menagerie*, the only American play in its repertoire.

We also had a couple of amateur stage performances to provide young people opportunities to develop acting skills. Some of my friends and I volunteered, hoping to impress the audience with our acting talents. I was given a small part, but it was long enough—all three or five minutes—to convince me that I would be better off remaining on the audience side of the curtain. Nevertheless, this experience didn't stop me from getting on stage again a few months later.

Instead of acting, I became involved in an innovative undertaking called *Elav Sõna* (The Living Word). The idea was to take the daily news releases from Reuters and other news agencies, translate them into Estonian, and have students read them live on stage to the news-hungry audience in the camp. The organizers approached my friend Heino and me with a proposal to do the reading.

"You can do it in the evening after school," they told us. "It would be a good public-speaking experience for you." Heino, who aspired to become an actor, accepted immediately, and I agreed to join him.

We received a typewritten copy of the day's news in the afternoon, leaving us a few hours to prepare for the evening reading. Occasionally, I had to consult with my mother for the correct pronunciation of certain foreign names because I didn't want to be embarrassed by mispronouncing the name of a Russian minister or a French movie star. Then we would step on stage and deliver the news, alternating between the two of us.

At the beginning our audience was small, but it grew steadily as word spread. Encouraged by its success, the program was expanded by adding other types of information: local camp news, opinion pieces by someone who had something interesting or provocative to say, interviews, humor, and poems. Sometimes we even had a singer or an instrumental artist to liven up the show. The expanded format made it necessary to move the program to the big hall in the *Gasthaus*, where we had a large stage with better lighting and bigger seating capacity. The increased size and scope of the program started to interfere with our homework, and eventually Heino and I were replaced by real actors, who could deliver a more professional performance.

Nowadays, when I watch the morning or evening news on television, I can't help but notice the striking similarity of these shows to the Living Word. The only difference is that we did it in front of a live audience, without cameras and commercial interruptions. I would like to think we were the true pioneers of news shows, long before they appeared on our television screens.

20

The Gates Are Opening

O N JUNE 25, 1948, an important event happened on the American side of the Atlantic Ocean that caught everyone's attention in the DP camps. President Harry S. Truman signed the Displaced Persons Act, which allowed refugees from Europe to immigrate to the United States beyond the original quotas set for their countries. For Estonians, that annual quota had been a scant 116. This limit, which had been in place for many years, had kept many of us from considering emigration to America. The removal of this barrier was the critical turning point that started the exodus of Estonians and other displaced persons to the United States.

Several countries had opened their doors to refugees earlier, but only to a select few for work in areas plagued by labor shortages. England was among the first to recruit single women for work in hospitals and sanatoriums. Several young women from Camp Bloherfelde applied and were accepted, among them a girl named Õie. She was a charming, blue-eyed brunette—a couple of years older than I—who lived across the hall from me. On the morning she left, a group of her friends and I got up at dawn to send her off with flowers and good wishes. Together with a few other girls, she left on a covered army truck, leaving us waving until the truck went out of sight. I was heartbroken. She was the love of my youth, my friend, and my favorite dance partner.

As more countries began to accept refugees, they, too, were shopping for healthy, young, and single individuals with specific skills: Belgium needed coal miners; Australia preferred farm workers; Canada was looking for lumberjacks; New Zealand wanted single women. Several South American countries, among them Argentina, Brazil, and Venezuela, also opened their gates to select groups of immigrants. The opportunities to leave Germany and start over in a foreign land created a huge amount of excitement in the camp. People gathered daily around the bulletin board looking for announcements on new emigration opportunities.

The early emigration offers for the DPs in the British Zone came from the British Commonwealth countries. Canada and Australia created the most interest because they were considered "lands of opportunity." Uncle Haakon was particularly intrigued by Canada, based on what he had heard from a couple of Canadian officers. The best job offers were for lumberjacks. The pay was excellent and once the men had settled, their families would be allowed to join them. He applied, but was rejected on the grounds of being overqualified. That didn't diminish his determination and he reapplied in the next hiring phase, omitting his law degree and work experience. This time he was accepted and the whole family moved to a transit camp in Fallingbostel (now Bad Fallingbostel) for screening and processing.

Uncle Karli was leaning toward Australia after he got a glowing report from a friend about opportunities in chicken farming there. He liked the idea of starting a farm and the fact that the whole family could go there together. His application was accepted and he was given preferred status because of his prior farming experience. Thus, he, Aunt Olli, and their toddler daughter Liis, bid us farewell and left for Fallingbostel, too.

Before he left, Uncle Karli asked me whether I would like to take over his tobacco business. When he explained how simple it was, I readily agreed. At first, my mother was a concerned because it seemed like black marketeering to her. But when she realized how much we could benefit from the extra income, she approved.

The last photo of our family before emigration

Uncle Karli introduced me to his supplier, gave me his customer list, storage containers, and a scale, and I was in business. Overnight, I became an entrepreneur at the young age of sixteen.

Running the business was easy. With a reliable supply of tobacco, it didn't take much effort to keep my customers satisfied. One day I had a knock on the door from a surprise customer. He was an upper-class teacher at my Gymnasium who lived in Camp Ohmstede.

"I understand that you have pipe tobacco for sale," he said.

My heart sank. I sensed possible trouble at school. "Ah … yes," I stammered.

"In that case, I would like to buy some."

"Of course," I replied with a sigh of relief. "How much do you need?"

I weighed the desired amount of tobacco, and we completed the transaction in uneasy silence. Then he thanked me, said good bye, and left without another word. He never came back.

As more and more people were leaving, I caught emigration fever like everyone else in the camp. Several of my classmates had already left—three for Australia and one for Canada. But any discussions with my mother about emigration ended quickly. "We are not going anywhere until you finish school," she said firmly. "There'll be no future for you without a Gymnasium diploma, no matter what country we go to." In fact, she already had a particular country in mind. "If we wait," she said, "we might be able to go to America. President Truman said that he wouldn't let us languish in camps forever." So we stayed and waited.

However, we couldn't remain in our camp much longer. A newly formed organization, the International Refugee Organization (IRO) took over responsibility for DP camps from UNRRA. It began to consolidate the camps and manage the emigration process. The vacancies left by emigrating families led to the closing of Camp Bloherfelde. It was a sad moment for everybody. It was particularly upsetting to lose the *Gasthaus*, where we had danced, played volleyball, and enjoyed countless concerts and theater performances. Some artists left for the American Zone to join the Estonian Theater in Geislingen, while the rest of the actors found a new home in Blomberg. Most of the remaining residents were transferred to Camp Sandplatz. My mother, and all others who were employed by the camp, lost their jobs and— more importantly—their valuable cigarette rations.

I loved the location of the new camp because it was within walking distance of my school and the city center. It was on the bank of a small canal where a former yacht club had built a small clubhouse and a boat dock. The clubhouse was an ideal place for reading magazines, playing chess, bridge, or other card games. A few steps away was a place for sunbathing and swimming, while farther down the stream anglers could catch fresh fish to augment their daily diet. On a few occasions, when the remains of a bombed-out bridge were demolished by explosives, they didn't even need a fishing rod. The stunned fish floated belly-up on the surface and everyone could wade into water and catch them with their bare hands.

Entrance to Camp Sandplatz

The living conditions at Camp Sandplatz were not much different from Camp Bloherfelde; it had the same type of dreary barracks, only spread out over a wider area. All the common facilities—offices, kitchen, and sauna—were similar. The outdoor sports facilities were somewhat better; it was only on cold winter days that I missed the indoor volleyball court in the Büsselmann's *Gasthaus*.

The barrack where I had lived in Camp Bloherfelde was dismantled and rebuilt at Camp Sandplatz. The work was mainly done by men who were former residents with the support of others when special expertise was required. Since school was out for the summer, my friends and I pitched in whenever our help was needed. I still remember the day when we were asked to help transport fiberglass insulation. We thought it would be fun to work with that fluffy stuff that looked like cotton candy, and went to work. After we had finished loading the truck, we climbed up and sank into the soft pile to rest in comfort on the way to our camp. It didn't take long before we started to itch. To our horror, we discovered that our unbearable skin irritation was caused by the tiny, almost invisible, fiberglass particles clinging to every inch of our sweaty bodies. It took several days of treatment—visits to the sauna and dispensary—to recover from our debilitating rashes. No wander the older men didn't want to touch that stuff.

When reconstruction was completed, all the former residents moved back from our temporary quarters. My mother, Grandmother, and I were happy to be in our room once again. If only my mother could find a job now, I thought, we would be even happier. Fortunately, she didn't have to wait very long. About a month later, the secretary of the camp emigrated to Australia, and my mother was offered her job in the office. She was delighted to be back at work and to receive her monthly cigarette allowance once again. My own tobacco business, started in Camp Bloherfelde, continued without interruption, and I even found several new customers.

One day I happened to meet a man who had a small workshop in a building next to ours. It was crammed with all kinds of electronic gadgets and components—everything from vacuum tubes and resistors to complete radio receivers. He was always tinkering with these devices. Noticing my interest in his work, he let me hang around and watch how he built and repaired radios. He explained how radios worked and gave me a couple of technical books to read. His own radio was usually tuned to music from a local radio station. When I told him how much I enjoyed the music, he gave me a tiny speaker, a switch, and a rheostat for volume control, and we connected them by a long pair of twisted wires to the radio amplifier in his shop. Suddenly, at the flip of a switch, our room was filled with music. Although the quality of sound was poor, and we were limited to his choice of music, it was better than boring silence. Luckily, my mother and Grandmother also happened to like his taste in music. And on those occasions when his radio was tuned to the news, we were able to stay up-to-date with the latest happenings in the world.

After losing several friends to emigration, I was eager to find new friends in Camp Sandplatz. I was particularly delighted to find two new table-tennis partners, Paul and Hans. Both of them were formidable challengers who made the sport interesting and enjoyable. Neither one was of my age.

Paul Kimmel was a married man in his late twenties. He and I became good friends and we attended many table-tennis tournaments in town together. Not only was he an outstanding athlete, he was one of a few people who could do anything well that interested him. He produced beautiful drawings and wood carvings and was terrific on the piano. His rendition of "Tiger Rag" still lingers in my memory. He emigrated to Australia where he died, unfortunately, at a fairly young age.

Hans Mirka was a twelve-year-old boy who was an exceptionally good player for his age. He was an aggressive player, smart, and very ambitious. When our paths crossed again twenty-five years later, he was a vice president at American Airlines.

On June 20, 1948, a major event occurred that affected everyone living in the occupied western zones—German citizens and DPs alike: a currency reform that replaced the previous reichsmark with the new deutschmark. The exchange rate was ten reichsmarks to one deutschmark. Only sixty reichsmarks per person could be exchanged evenly for sixty deutschmarks. It was the end of the "cigarette economy." Suddenly, my mother's salary became more important than her cigarette rations. Almost overnight, store shelves were filled with goods we hadn't seen for a long time. It was good news for the German economy, but bad news for my business. With cigarettes and tobacco readily available at stores everywhere, I had no choice but to close my business and start looking for new challenges.

I always wanted to learn how to drive an automobile and considered myself ready for it at the ripe age of seventeen. One of my friends was Harald Põhi, a driver for IRO who delivered supplies and transported people. He kept his small Fordson army truck at the camp between his driving assignments and, on rainy days, he drove me and my friends to school. He was also willing to give me driving lessons. For many days, he let me sit in the driver's seat of his parked truck to practice shifting gears, and he explained how everything from the dashboard to the shifting mechanism worked. Finally, after my persistent pleadings, he let me take the wheel and slowly drive around the camp. For a real driving experience, he took me to quiet country roads after dark for clandestine driving lessons in a Volkswagen bug. It was a daring adventure—we both knew that his job was at risk for giving the controls to an unauthorized driver without a license. In those days driving was more complicated than it is nowadays because it required double clutching when shifting into lower gear. Harald would sit patiently at my side—biting his fingernails—until he was satisfied that I was able to shift gears without grinding the gearbox.

I also learned to play bridge that summer. My interest in the game was roused by watching the players at the clubhouse. When one of them explained the rules of the game to me and my friends, we quickly formed an enthusiastic foursome. We played by the Culbertson's rules, the most popular system at that time, since Goren's point-counting system had not yet arrived in Europe. Once we had caught on to the finer details of the game, we became practically addicted, playing for hours almost every day during the summer. I am not sure whether we enjoyed the game for the mental challenge or for the feeling that we had arrived in the adult world.

My new passion for bridge left me no time for chess, a game that I used to play in the early days in Camp Bloherfelde. I had even participated in a tournament when the Estonian chess master Ortvin Sarapuu visited our camp and played simultaneously against a large number of opponents. It was a memorable experience. I was struck by his ability to move quickly from one player to the next, checkmating one after another. Thus, my early surrender came as no surprise. Years later, I learned that he had emigrated to New Zealand, shortened his name to Sarapu, and later earned the Chess International Master title.

With increasing emigration opportunities, people began to prepare themselves for possible life in a new country. We realized that it was not only essential to know the language, it was equally important to develop certain skills to meet a particular country's needs. English language and vocational courses were most popular. They were taught by resident experts to anyone who was interested. I signed up for a technical drawing course, thinking that it might help me in case I wanted to become an architect. I spent countless hours with men between their twenties and fifties, learning how to draw lines of different widths and shapes and how to use stencils for lettering. Although I never became an architect, the course did help me get my first job in America.

Despite the fact that the Displaced Persons Act had been signed in 1948, emigration to the United States didn't begin until the following year. It was a disappointment for those who had declined other opportunities in the hope of prompt departure to the United States. The delay, however, was a blessing for me because it gave me enough time to finish Gymnasium and thereby satisfy my mother's precondition for emigration. To accommodate emigrating students, the school went on an accelerated schedule, curtailed summer recess, and increased school hours. Any student who was scheduled to emigrate before graduation day, had completed 120 school days and maintained good grades, qualified for a diploma. For me, it meant that I could graduate and leave as early as September 1949.

Encouraged by this policy, my mother began pursuing emigration to America. The process was not as easy as we had expected. First, one needed a guarantor who could provide assurance that the emigrant's family would have housing and employment upon arrival in the United States. There were two types of assurances. The first was for a specific individual or a family by name; the other was "anonymous"—an offer for a specified number of workers who could meet the sponsor's requirements. The California Farmer's Association was one sponsor that offered jobs to one hundred DPs to work in orange groves in Cucamonga, California. Picking oranges was not my mother's idea of making a living, so she contacted an old friend of Grandmother's, a long-time resident of New York City, for help in finding a sponsor for us.

While we waited for a sponsor, I prepared myself for life in America. Although I had always been interested in everything about the United States, the prospect of actually going there intensified my curiosity. I read as many American books and magazines as I could find, hoping to discover what America was all about. Among other

interesting facts I learned that Americans love to play golf and drink
martinis. In one magazine I found an article that caught my particular
attention. It featured a story about a university in New York City,
called Columbia. I liked the majestic look of the historic buildings
and was impressed by its academic reputation and Ivy League tradition. Even though I was aware of the fame of Harvard University,
Columbia became the university of my dreams. It seemed an impossible dream at that time, but it lingered on in my mind until eight years
later, when I did walk through its majestic gates as a graduate student.

Some additional tidbits of information about the American lifestyle came from my pen pal, Diana, a high school student in Sche-
nectady, New York. I don't recall how our correspondence started,
but most likely it was arranged through the YMCA. It provided a
great opportunity to practice letter-writing in English and learn what
students of my age were doing in America. Unfortunately, our correspondence didn't last very long. It came to an abrupt end when I
wrote her that I was going to America and might even be able to meet
her. I didn't receive a reply. The thought of actually confronting a
displaced person face-to-face may have frightened her and her family.

Meanwhile, letters started to arrive from Canada. Upon his arrival
in Halifax, Uncle Haakon had been assigned to a group of men that
would work in the forests of Mattawa in Saskatchewan province. The
men found the northern Canadian winter incredibly harsh, even
though they had grown up in the Nordic Estonian climate. They
worked seven days a week—five days for the company and two days
for themselves—building homes for their families, who were waiting
to join them, much like American homesteaders had done a century
earlier. By working in teams, they built one house at a time, and when
it was completed, they started on the next one, until all the families
were reunited in a home of their own.

Uncle Karli's family, waiting in a transit camp for passage to
Australia, was struck by a serious setback. Their one-year-old daughter, Liis, had contracted meningitis. Having lost their only son at an
early age, the parents were desperate with the dread of losing their
daughter, too. The doctors were helpless since the only cure—the new

"wonder drug" penicillin that had been used for treating wounded American soldiers in the battlefield—was not available for civilians. A worldwide emergency call by the Red Cross helped find a source for the medicine and that saved the life of Liis.

Her illness caused the family to miss their scheduled departure for Australia. As they waited for the next transport, they had time to reconsider their emigration plans. The news from friends who had emigrated to Australia was no longer encouraging. Initial enthusiasm had subsided; many families felt isolated and had problems adjusting to their new environment. All of a sudden, America became a better option. They changed their minds and applied for a visa to the United States.

My mother was overjoyed by their decision. "I am so glad they're going to America," she said. "Now our families will be on the same continent. I never understood what attracted them to Australia in the first place."

As the emigrations gained momentum, more small DP camps were closed and the remaining Estonians were transferred to either Oldenburg or Lingen, the two major DP centers left for us in the British Zone. It was the beginning of the end of the DP era.

During those years, while we were struggling to survive, the military and civilian administrators of the camps enjoyed a good life. They had many privileges and money that went far in the German economy. They were often invited to parties where they found young women eager to win their friendship. I remember my mother telling me about the Australian major in charge of our camp who came to her office one day with a dejected look on his face. He sat on a chair, buried his face in his hands, and sighed, "My good life is coming to an end."

"What's happening?" my mother asked. "Are you being sent back to Australia?"

"Oh, no. Not at all. My wife is coming over here."

My mother, knowing his reputation as a ladies' man, understood him well. But as more and more DPs were leaving Germany, the camps were being closed, and the major, too, would have to ready himself to leave Germany.

21

Coming to America

I T WAS A warm summer day in late August when my mother came running, waving a white envelope in her hand. I never believed that I would see my mother, who was always an exemplar of proper behavior, skipping like giddy teenage girl. I knew immediately that she was bringing good news.

Unable to control her excitement, she blurted out, "We are going to America." Then she collapsed on a chair, gasped for breath, and announced proudly, "I have a sponsor who wants me to work as a live-in maid for a family in New York."

"This is great." I said. "But what about me?"

"You just turned eighteen. You can still come as my dependent."

"Fantastic!" I shouted, examining the letter. "So we are really going to America!"

As soon as I had recovered from my euphoria, I began to have second thoughts. "This job," I said. "Working as a housemaid? Is this really right for you? Back home, before the Russians came, you had a housemaid who worked for you. Besides, are you even strong enough to do that kind of work?"

"If this is what it takes to get to America, I will do it," was my mother's resolute answer. "Jobs like this are the only opportunities for single women. This is a good deal. It includes food and lodging as well. Look, it is only for one year. After that, I can find a better job."

"So when can we leave?" I asked.

"We should be ready to leave for the transit camp in about a week. I need to clear the office and start packing as soon as possible."

The next day I shared the good news with my classmates and notified the school's principal. He confirmed that I qualified for a diploma and promised to forward it to me.

When the army truck arrived to take us to the transit camp, we were ready with our suitcases filled with clothes, a few valuables, and some family memorabilia. From my sparse, worn-out wardrobe, I had chosen only the items worth keeping, hoping to buy new American-style clothes soon after our arrival in New York.

My mother had made sure we possessed all the necessary documents. She had a notarized affidavit stating that her marital status was "separated," the official status of women whose husbands' whereabouts were unknown after their arrest by the Soviets. Nearly ten years later, we were still trying to learn the fate of my father, whether was he was dead or alive. My mother had another notarized document listing all the valuables we had brought from Estonia: a silver-trimmed crystal plate, some silver dinnerware, a gold necklace, bracelet, brooch, and her wedding ring.

Saying good-bye to my grandmother was the hardest part of leaving. She remained behind, waiting to join Aunt Senta's family in Canada. During the time she'd stayed with us in the camp, I'd learned to appreciate everything she had done for my mother and me. Although I had occasionally rebelled against her telling me what to do and what not to do, I now wish I had paid more attention to her advice. Her opinions on diet and exercise—particularly stretching and breathing—were uncannily close to what health experts recommend today. She was a smart, strong woman who had endured her wartime tragedies with courage and poise. As we said good-bye to her, we had no doubt that she would be able to manage well without us.

Our first destination was Camp Wentorf, twelve miles east of Hamburg, with a bureaucratic-sounding name at its entrance: Regional Resettlement Processing Center. It had been converted from a German Army base to a transit camp for DPs of various nationalities who were waiting to leave for the country of their dreams, the United States of America.

As soon as we passed the gate, I noticed that the camp was unlike the DP camps in Oldenburg. Instead of dreary wooden barracks, there were well-constructed two- and three-story buildings along tree-lined streets, along with the sidewalks that characterize many small German towns. Inside the buildings, however, the picture was less pleasant. Families and their belongings were crammed into small spaces, separated from each other by blankets that served as makeshift room dividers. Yet, everyone seemed to take it in stride. After all, it was a temporary inconvenience on the way to a better life.

Our biggest concern was the screening process performed by the IRO staff members. They were the official gatekeepers who controlled our future, deciding who could enter the United States or who should be left behind. In addition to having a legitimate sponsor, one had to be in good health, and be politically acceptable. People with criminal records, communists, and Nazi collaborators were rejected.

The screening started with a medical examination that included an X-ray and blood tests. Anyone with tuberculosis or a venereal disease was disqualified. My mother was noticeably worried, and for good reason—she had suffered tuberculosis in her youth. Although she was in good health after having been fully cured by a novel treatment, she was afraid to disclose her bout with the disease. She decided to remain silent, hoping and praying that she would pass the X-ray test. I was equally nervous and kept my fingers crossed as I left her in the line for the X-ray exam.

When Mother returned, she was flabbergasted. "The doctor was completely baffled," she said. "There was a void on the X-ray image by my right lung. He didn't know what to make of it. When he asked if I have had TB, I replied, 'No.' Then he went to consult another doctor. He came back a few minutes later, stamped my card without saying a word, and wished me good luck."

Still in a slight daze, she put her arm around me and exclaimed, "Thank God, we can go to America now." What a relief! She had just cleared the most worrisome hurdle on our way to the United States.

My medical exam was more routine than my mother's. All men had to stand naked before the examining doctor, with their arms raised above their heads. In addition to a general health check, they examined our armpits, looking for blood-group tattoos to identify men who had served in the Waffen-SS during the war. Even my armpit didn't escape the curious look of the examiner, despite the fact that I was only fourteen when the war ended.

My ID card issued at Camp Wentorf

With the medical examinations behind us, we still needed a couple of mandatory immunizations before the Medical Officer would put a final-approval stamp on our ID cards. Still more approvals were required from the Documentation Officer, the Security Officer, and the Consul's representative. We spent countless hours waiting in lines and filling out forms about our personal history. The bureaucratic process was incredibly slow and frustrating. Someone joked that you'd be ready to go only when the weight of the paperwork exceeded your own weight. It was only after we had passed all the screenings and had all the proper stamps on our ID cards that we could finally relax. From that moment on, it was only a matter of time as to when we would be assigned to a ship bound for the United States.

I passed the time playing table tennis and volleyball during the day and dancing in the evening. There were always some musicians ready to play and enough young people eager to court and engage the opposite sex in a foxtrot or a tango on the dance floor.

We were not allowed to leave the camp because of a recent polio outbreak; officials didn't want us to carry the disease aboard the ships and eventually to the United States. But since this restriction wasn't rigorously enforced, I was able go with a couple of friends for a day trip to Hamburg. We roamed about the city like typical tourists, taking photos and visiting a few historical sites that had survived the wartime bombings. We even walked by the famous red-light district, where we witnessed the British Military Police chasing hapless pleasure-seeking soldiers in a surprise raid.

After two weeks of waiting, we received orders to leave for the final transit camp near the port of our departure, Bremerhaven. It was a memorable train ride. Everyone was in high spirits. I traveled in the company of two Estonian students, Hans Kobin and Richard (Riks) Pertel from Baltic University, which was established shortly after the war by former professors from the Baltic States. They told me about their exciting life as university students and introduced me to an age-old student tradition of celebrating important occasions with a shot of vodka. The trip certainly was an occasion worth celebrating. Life was good!

Camp Grohn provided temporary housing for emigrants waiting for the next ship to the United States. As soon as we arrived, we were ushered to the dining room for lunch. I was amazed by the brightly lit, cafeteria-style kitchen and the abundant variety of food. There was fresh orange juice, milk, ham, eggs, potatoes, and plenty of ice cream to finish the feast. That was the best camp food I have ever had.

The camp had separate living quarters for men and women. The men's rooms had rows of three-tiered bunk beds. My new friends and I commandeered a bunk next to a wall, which offered some degree of privacy. I ended up on the middle bunk, which was deemed the least desirable. "On that bunk," they joked, "you need both an umbrella and a gas mask." It was a good omen that we were going to get along splendidly in the days ahead. We discovered that we all liked to play bridge, and as soon we found a fourth hand, we were playing almost around the clock, using a suitcase as a makeshift card table.

On October 3, 1949, we were informed that we should be ready by the next morning for the train to Bremenhaven, the embarkation point for our long-awaited journey. After breakfast, my bridge companions and I decided to remain in the building and play the last few hands before joining the others who were waiting outside for the train. It was a good game and we didn't stop playing until the train arrived.

When my mother finally saw me coming down, she was not amused. She had been searching the whole assembly area and, unable to find me, was worried that I might miss the train, as I almost had in Danzig five years earlier. She couldn't understand why I had to play bridge all that time, though I thought it was a neat way to act like a savvy traveler and avoid the frenzied crowd of travelers. Besides, I told her, one doesn't say "no" to friends who are short of a fourth bridge player.

The train took us directly to the harbor where our "cruise liner," the *USS General Hersey,* was docked. It was one of the many Liberty ships that were mass produced for transporting American troops during the war.

When we arrived in our assigned quarters, we found a maze of steel pipes that supported four levels of stretched canvas bunks, about two feet wide and six feet long. The vertical spacing between the bunks was so tight that if you bent your knees, you would hit the person above you. The ceiling fans circulated stale air reeking of garlic and motor oil. With our baggage stacked in the narrow aisles between the bunks, there was hardly any room to move around. That claustrophobic dungeon was going to be our habitat for the next ten days at sea. Hans, Riks, and I took the lower three bunks on the nearest stack, leaving the top one for a man from Poland. The women's quarters where my mother stayed were more suitable for human beings. They were less crowded, and the bunks were only two levels high.

Embarking *USS General Hersey* in Bremenhafen

Once settled, we went on deck to watch the ship pull away from the dock and to get a last glimpse of Germany. The traditional European ritual is to send off sailing ships with music and bravado, and our ship did not escape such a farewell celebration. A typical German oom-pah band was on the dock blasting waltzes, polkas, and some of the latest popular tunes. It seemed that the band had just discovered the Brazilian samba rhythm, judging from their passionate rendition of "Ai, ai, ai Maria, Maria von Bahia" as we pulled away from the dock.

Immediately following the lifeboat drill, all men were assigned to various work details. Hans and Riks were sent to work in the PX store, while I was assigned to "can detail" with several other men. None of us knew what "can detail" meant until we reported for duty the next morning. An officer explained that our job was to go through the ship every morning and collect all trash cans and dump their contents overboard. Not exactly the most pleasant assignment, but a consolation was that we could finish our chore in about half an hour, after which we were free for the rest of the day. Fortunately, the cans were emptied early in the morning when hardly anyone was around to see me performing this undignified chore. When someone asked me about my mysterious assignment, I remarked smugly that I was on "can detail."

At sunset, the captain got on the loudspeaker to inform us that we had entered the English Channel. Everyone rushed to the starboard side to get a glimpse of the English coast. Although it was growing dark, we were close enough to see occasional automobiles driving along the seaside road. I lingered on the railing to have one last glimpse of Europe's rocky terrain until it disappeared into darkness.

Soon afterward, the captain hollered another message: "I am pleased to announce that we will arrive in New York on October 12th, the day when Christopher Columbus landed in America in 1492. In the United States, we celebrate that day as a holiday and call it Columbus Day." After the message had been translated to those who didn't understand English, a cheer broke out on the deck. We could not have found a more fitting day to arrive in the country of our dreams.

Pleasant weather during the early days of the voyage allowed me to spend most of my days on deck. With no one available to play bridge—Hans and Riks were busy selling snacks and toiletries in the PX—I had plenty of free time to roam around and relish the fresh ocean air. A couple of times a day I visited my mother, whose stomach seemed to have an aversion to the ship's heaving and rolling motions. I made sure she came out to the deck for fresh air and had something to eat from the mess hall. The rest of the time I would read, talk to fellow passengers, and hang out with two Estonian girls from Baltic University.

One afternoon, an officer invited the girls to the officers' clubroom later that evening. The girls, hesitant to go by themselves, invited me to join them. I was glad to oblige. When the three of us showed up at the clubroom door, the surprised look on the host's face showed that he certainly hadn't expected me. However, he was very gracious and invited me in as well. He was a tall, sturdy man, clad in a khaki uniform, with a round face—a sharp contrast to the lean bodies and undernourished faces I was used to seeing in Germany. He introduced us to two other officers, similarly portly, with fleshy faces. I began to wonder whether all men in America looked like that.

Enjoying fresh air and pleasant company on deck

The clubroom was a luxurious oasis in the middle of our floating vessel, reminding me of fancy hotel lounges I had seen in Hollywood movies. The carpeted room had cushioned lounge chairs clustered around a couple of cocktail tables. The soft lights and jazz music helped me forget that I was aboard a ship. Only the slight heave of the ocean waves reminded me that I was at sea.

We were served snacks with drinks, and the officers talked about life in America. They apologized for our crowded living quarters and added, "This is not as bad as it was when the ship was transporting troops during the war. There were three times as many soldiers on board, the bunks were five tiers high, and many men slept on the open deck."

Fifty-five years later, when I crossed the Atlantic in the opposite direction, from New York to Southampton on the cruise liner *Queen Mary 2*, I couldn't help thinking back to this trip. How dramatically different these two voyages were. The crossing on the *Queen Mary 2* took half as much time, the passengers traveled in luxury on the upper decks, and the crew slept in crowded cabins on the lower decks.

Several days into the voyage, Mother Nature had a surprise for us. She engulfed us in a major storm in the middle of the Atlantic Ocean. The ship tossed and heaved like a toy boat in a swimming pool, making life miserable for everyone. Most of the passengers were seasick and the appalling air in the cabins made the suffering even worse. We were cautioned against going on deck because of the wind and lashing waves. However, the work of the can detail had to be done, no matter how challenging the task. Several members of the detail were seasick and failed to show up, leaving me with a skeleton team to cope with the exceptionally heavy cans. In addition to the usual trash of candy wrappers, tissues, and cigarette butts, they now contained the waste of seasick passengers. It was a giant struggle to drag the foul-smelling cans to the railing and heave them overboard without getting ourselves blown out to sea. The work required not only physical strength, but also careful planning. It was very important to avoid being downwind while tipping the can. I felt sorry for one poor fellow who learned that lesson the hard way. When our job was finished, I considered my passage from Bremerhaven to America fully paid.

After breakfast, I brought some light food from the mess hall to my mother who, like most of the passengers, was suffering from seasickness and was unable to leave her bunk. I, on the other hand, actually loved going to the mess hall during the storm. There were no waiting lines, I could have as many scrambled eggs as my heart desired, and the supply of ice cream was unlimited.

The storm lasted for a couple of days, adding a two-day delay to our journey. Instead of arriving in New York on Columbus Day, we landed in Boston on October 14, 1949. It was a beautiful sunny day. Practically everyone was on deck trying to catch the first sight of the land that was about to become our new home. The sense of energy and excitement was palpable. I had never seen such a crowd of ecstatic people, chatting and shouting in many different languages. Several people tossed their hats and some small items overboard as a symbolic ritual of leaving our fears and anxieties behind. Caught by their frenzy, I, too, grabbed my shabby fedora and, with great bravura, tossed it into the water. Brimming with hope and optimism, we looked forward to entering the New World.

The first people greeting us on American soil were uniformed men with wide-brimmed cowboy hats, who looked very much like the cowboys I had seen in western movies. But their blue-grey uniforms and polished boots belied their cowboy image; they were local state troopers making sure that everyone went through the immigration process. Representatives of several faith-based aid organizations were also present and ready to help. Because most Estonians are Lutherans, we were welcomed by World Lutheran Federation workers. Each new arrival received two dollars of spending money and a train ticket to a final destination, to be repaid within three months.

My mother and I were among a large group of people taken to the railroad station to board a train bound for New York. As soon as we entered the train, we were greeted by attendants enticing us to spend our newly acquired wealth on drinks and snacks. My first purchase in America, as for many others in our group, was a bottle of ice-cold Coca-Cola. Next, I bought a fresh orange and cookies for my mother, who was still recovering from the effects of the storm.

Suddenly, a loud argument broke out between the vendors and a newly arrived American. I heard someone with a heavy accent raise his voice, "We just arrived, and they're already trying to take advantage of us." A disgruntled man, counting the change in the palm of his hand that he had just received for his purchase—two quarters, one dime, and one nickel—complained, "I was supposed to get sixty-five cents, but he gave me only fifty-six cents. I want the nine cents he owes me."

The vendor, indignant at being accused of cheating, counted the change and explained that a dime was worth ten cents.

"But it says 'one' on it," insisted the man, pointing at the coin.

"It is a dime and it's worth ten cents," repeated the vendor. "Do you understand? *Capiche?*"

"Are you sure?"

"Yes, it is true, a dime is worth ten cents," confirmed another vendor.

"It is a crazy system," said the man, shaking his head as he returned to his seat.

The train arrived at Pennsylvania Station in New York City late in the evening. As we stepped off the train, we glanced over the platform and tried to find our sponsors. We really didn't know how to look for them. We only knew that they were Mr. and Mrs. Newberg from Woodmere, Long Island. A helpful World Lutheran Federation representative finally brought us together. Mr. Newberg was a distinguished-looking middle-aged man in a dark blue suit, wearing horn-rimmed glasses. Mrs. Newberg was a small, slender, dark-haired lady, a perfect match to her advertising-executive husband. They hired a porter to take our baggage to their car—the most luxurious car I had ever seen. I was impressed by its quiet ride and plush interior. My biggest surprise was that Mr. Newberg didn't need to shift gears, as the transmission was all automatic. I tried to get a glimpse of the surroundings in the darkness, but all I could see were rows of automobile headlights streaming toward us on an incredibly wide highway.

After about a half-hour ride we reached our sponsor's home, a two-story Tudor-style house in a quiet, tree-lined neighborhood. We met their two teenage sons, David and Larry, whose curious looks told me that they were surprised to see me. Mrs. Newberg showed us my mother's room: a bed, a small table and a chair, a dresser with a mirror, an alarm clock, and a radio.

"With your own bathroom you will have plenty of privacy here," she explained. Then she looked at me, pointed at a folding rollaway bed, and said, "You can stay here too until you find a job."

Her unambiguous message, that I was expected soon to be on my own, left me with mixed emotions. On the one hand, I cherished the idea of living independently, away from my mother's watchful eye. I had finished Gymnasium and considered myself ready for the adult world. On the other hand, the prospect of finding a job and a place to live in a strange country seemed rather scary. Where would I start? Where could I find help, if needed? But then, I thought, why worry? This was the beginning of the biggest adventure of my life. Most immigrants before me had succeeded, and so would I.

It was well past midnight when I collapsed on the rollaway bed. After sleeping ten nights on a piece of stretched canvas, it felt as luxurious as a four-poster bed made for royalty. My head was spinning from all the recent events. It was hard to believe how lucky I had been to come so far. The perilous years of my life had finally reached an end. For the first time, I felt truly safe, separated by the wide Atlantic Ocean from a Europe that was still endangered by the threat of Soviet Russia. I am in a free country now, I thought, full of opportunities that no dictator can deny me, and where no bombs or bullets can stop me. I am in America.

Epilogue

MY FIRST JOB interview in America was at Mount Sinai Hospital in New York City. It ended with a mutual agreement that I was not the right person to work as a hospital orderly. As I left the building and strolled down Fifth Avenue, I noticed an unusually large police presence and a rapidly growing crowd, buzzing excitedly as if waiting for something important to happen. Since I was in no hurry, I decided to stop and wait. The next thing I saw was a slow-moving formation of police motorcycles, followed by an open convertible in which stood a man of a medium height, with glasses, waving to the cheering crowd. That man was none other than Harry S. Truman, the President of the United States, the same man who had signed the Displaced Persons Act, which had made it possible for me to be here. "Thank you, Mr. President," I whispered and waved. I couldn't believe my luck. I had been in the country for only one week and already I had seen the president! This must be a good omen, I thought. That turned out to be true.

One week later, I landed a job with a surveyor, Quentin F. Disher, whose office was within walking distance of the Newbergs' home. When Mrs. Newberg heard that I had gotten the job because of my mathematics skills, she said, "David hasn't been doing well in his math class. If you could help him with his homework, you can stay with us." This generous offer was all that I needed. With a weekly $25 salary and free room and board at the Newbergs, I could easily make ends meet. My mother was also pleased about this unexpected turn of events.

Mr. Disher kept me busy with added responsibilities and soon I was making $30 a week. That income allowed me to save enough money to enter Upsala College in New Jersey the following year. I enrolled as a junior because a European Gymnasium education was considered equivalent to the first two years of college in America. With a small scholarship and part-time and summer work with Mr. Disher, I was able to graduate two years later with a BS degree in mathematics and a physics minor.

My mother continued to work for the Newberg family until she completed her one-year obligation. Uncle Karli, who had been working for his sponsor at an estate in Ohio, moved to Long Island and bought a two-family house, where his family and my mother settled down. She was self-employed for a while, until she got a job as quality-control inspector at a pharmaceutical firm. She later went to work in the accounting department of the Girl Scouts of America, where she stayed until her retirement.

Eventually, Grandmother was able to join Aunt Senta's family in Canada. They moved from frigid Mattawa to St. Catherines, Ontario, near the U.S. border, where Uncle Haakon worked for the Ontario Hydro Company and later joined a legal firm as a law clerk; he remained there until his retirement. Their children, Andres and Marike, both became schoolteachers and raised eight children between them. Aunt Senta began corresponding with one of her friends in Estonia who provided us information about the fate of our relatives behind the iron curtain. It was through that contact that I first learned about my father's death in Siberia.

After graduation from Upsala, I gave up my dream of becoming an architect and decided to pursue further studies in electrical engineering. I applied for scholarships at twenty-five universities and received two offers. I accepted an offer of free tuition from the Worcester Polytechnic Institute in Massachusetts, and by living in and working part-time at a funeral home, completed my studies in two years, earning a second BS degree in electrical engineering.

Soon thereafter, I was drafted into the U.S. Army. It didn't come as a surprise because my deferment as a college student had expired upon graduation. Since the hostilities of the Korean War had already ended, I didn't have to go overseas to face the bombs and bullets of another war. I completed my two years of service as an electronics specialist entirely in the United States. Still, I was qualified a Korean War veteran and became eligible for financial aid for further education through the GI Bill. With that support, and with part-time work at IBM, I was able at long last to fulfill my dream of studying at Columbia University. Two years later, I graduated with a master's degree in electrical engineering, ready for a full-time career in industry.

I joined the Sperry Gyroscope Company in Long Island, NY, where I worked on developing remotely controlled aircraft systems, forerunners of the drones used in present-day warfare.

In the evenings after work, I spent most of my free time with my Estonian friends who had—like many newly arrived immigrants—settled in the New York area. A common meeting place was the Estonian House, a popular clubhouse in midtown Manhattan, where many social and cultural activities took place. At one of those events I met an attractive, rather shy student from City College named Siret Jaanus. She intrigued me because she was more serious and thoughtful than many other girls I dated. We had gone out only a couple of times when the burgeoning aerospace industry on the West Coast beckoned. In the summer of 1961, I received an attractive job offer from the Autonetics Division of North American Aviation at its brand new Anaheim facility in California. It was an offer I could not refuse.

I left my mother and all the girls, including Siret, behind and moved to Anaheim, the town synonymous with Disneyland. It was a move I have never regretted. I loved the Southern California climate and lifestyle and, above all, I enjoyed working with a team of highly talented colleagues on the leading edge of digital computing. I liked the stimulating environment and I was proud to make a contribution to the defense of the United States and the free world. After working four years as a senior engineer, I was promoted into management, where I held a variety of leadership positions until my retirement in 1990.

At an office party in 1969, I happened to meet a young lady named Linda Staggs. Her good looks and charming smile captivated me immediately. Following a whirlwind romance, we got married six months later. Our honeymoon period was not much longer than our courtship. After seven months of marriage, we discovered that we weren't compatible and decided to get divorced. At least we proved the naysayers wrong, those who predicted that the marriage wouldn't last more than six months.

Two years later, I was attending an Estonian theater performance in Toronto, Canada, when during intermission I stumbled while passing a row of seats. As I turned to apologize, I saw a pair of deep brown eyes—eyes I had seen somewhere before.

"Siret, is that you?" I asked in amazement.

Yes, indeed, it was Siret Jaanus, the girl whom I had dated before I left New York. No longer the insecure young girl I remembered, she was now a young woman with poise and confidence. She had recently received a PhD degree in pharmacology from a medical school and was teaching at the State University of New York School of Optometry.

When she told me she was going to attend a conference in California in three weeks, I asked her to call me. She did, and we spent several days enjoying the best of what Southern California had to offer—from a concert at the Hollywood Bowl to a bullfight in Tijuana, Mexico. After that week, every one of my business trips to the east coast included a weekend side trip to New York. We had an exciting cross-continent romance. I proposed to her on New Year's Eve of 1972 and we had a June wedding the following year in New York City. The romance that had started with a chance encounter in Toronto is still alive after more than forty-two years of marriage.

In order to deal with increased management responsibilities, Autonetics sponsored me for an Executive MBA program at Claremont Graduate University, where I attended classes at night and on weekends. There I had the opportunity to meet Peter Drucker, the great management visionary who is often called the "father of modern management." His teachings left an indelible mark on me and influenced me to continue working with a stimulating faculty that included another great scholar, Paul Gray, my thesis advisor for a doctorate in management and a dear friend.

Siret and I on our thirtieth wedding anniversary

The PhD degree opened doors for me in academia, and immediately after my retirement from Autonetics, I was offered a tenure-track faculty position at Fordham University Graduate School of Business in New York City. I accepted and, for more than a decade, Siret and I enjoyed the bustling big-city life of Manhattan. I devoted my time to research and teaching, while Siret went back to teaching at her former school. I found a new passion in teaching and sharing my knowledge with the next generation of managers and business leaders. It was one of the most rewarding experiences of my life.

Eventually, the sunny southern California climate lured us back to a more relaxed lifestyle in the seaside community of Corona del Mar. Though I continued to teach part-time for a while, I also traveled and devoted time to writing and reflecting on my life's experiences.

Our travels have taken us to many interesting places in Europe, Asia, and the Middle East. We've met people of different nationalities and cultures but have also taken time to visit places from my past. We were pleasantly surprised to see how fast West German cities had erased their scars of war and were now bustling with vitality. But the cities that had been behind the Iron Curtain before German reunification were different. When I returned to Jena in 2001, I could find hardly anything recognizable in the heavily bombed city center; in its place were plazas, greenbelts, and parking lots. The apartment house where I used to live looked unchanged except for its adjoining twin building: destroyed in an air raid, it had been rebuilt—not in its original design, but in an entirely different, modern architectural style. Sadly, I was unable to locate anyone who could tell me what had happened since I had left. Young people were too young, and the old couldn't remember or didn't want to talk about their painful past.

The most gratifying visits were to my homeland, Estonia. Since my first visit in 1994, I have been back there more than ten times. The progress the country has made during that period has been remarkable. It has adopted free-market economic policies, privatized formerly state-owned enterprises, and introduced a flat-rate income tax. Its economy is now almost debt free, and, scored on economic freedom, is rated second in Europe. By joining the European Union, NATO, and adopting the euro as its currency, Estonia is now firmly integrated with other European countries.

The best part of my early visits was catching up with Cousins Eda and Ilmar after half a century of absence. We spent endless hours talking, rummaging for old photos and memorabilia, and reminiscing about our childhood days. Despite being deported to Siberia on two occasions, they did not complain about their past misfortunes but were happy to be back in their home. It was always a pure joy to be with them.

One afternoon, Siret, Eda, and I walked past the house where I had lived during my early childhood years. I introduced myself to the couple in the front yard as a former resident of their home and asked permission to photograph the house. "Of course you can," said the lady and cordially extended her hand. "I'm so delighted to meet you. We've always been curious about the history of this house." They invited us in, showed us the house, and walked us through the yard. On the outside it looked exactly as I remembered it; only the interior had been renovated, in a tasteful modern style. Afterwards, we had tea and cookies with the whole family—a lovely couple with two delightful teenage daughters. A few days later, we were invited for a dinner in their backyard. It was a memorable evening; I could never have imagined that I would be drinking wine and eating barbecued ribs on the site of my childhood sandbox. I am pleased that the house is now home to such a nice family. They are dear friends who enrich our visits to Tallinn, which have become annual rituals for us.

People who have heard me talk about my experiences during the war often ask, "How did you manage to survive it all?"

"Luck," I would answer. "I was just lucky."

However, countless people from the Baltic States were not as fortunate. Many perished in bomb attacks or died in Soviet prison camps; others suffered nearly five decades of repression under Soviet occupation. I was lucky to escape the deportations to Siberia, lucky to flee on the last train ahead of the Soviet tanks, and lucky to be in the main air-raid bunker instead of a restaurant shelter where everyone was buried alive. I was also lucky to have had good parents who lovingly raised me to value integrity, ambition, and honor. They gave me good genes that have allowed me to reach an advanced age, with time to sit back and view my life in retrospect.

I have learned that luck alone does not guarantee success. The famous French chemist Louis Pasteur once said that chance prefers a prepared mind. With that statement he brilliantly described the role of luck in our lives and the importance of being prepared to recognize and take advantage of opportunities when they arise. Good education and training can prepare us for life's uncertainties. For example, my mother was prepared for the post-war period because she had already mastered several languages but also because she took typing classes after our arrival in Germany.

Many people mistakenly believe that money guarantees success in life. In turbulent times, it is possible to lose one's wealth almost overnight, as evidenced by stock-market crashes, currency devaluations, and bankruptcies. Countless Estonians, including my family and relatives, lost their businesses, jobs, homes, and life savings during the Soviet occupation of Estonia. The only possessions that the occupiers couldn't take away were our minds—the knowledge and wisdom we had accumulated through education and experience. People who spoke foreign languages and possessed some practical skills were better able to survive and start new lives, even under the most difficult circumstances. Knowledge is the most precious and everlasting asset that a person can have.

Another factor that enabled us to survive the terrible times during the war was perseverance—the ability to endure and persist in spite of all difficulties. The Finnish people have a word for it—they call it *sisu*. It is an inner strength of will, determination and tenacity in the face of adversity, "having guts," to put it succinctly. *Sisu* is often used to describe the Finnish character. I do believe that Estonians, being closely related to Finns, have plenty of *sisu* in our character as well.

People with *sisu* tend to be optimists by nature. I still remember how my father used the story of two frogs to illustrate the importance of optimism. That simple story has often reminded me to see the brighter side of every situation. I believe that by being an optimist like my father, I have been able to endure the most difficult times in my life.

Living in a displaced persons' camp in close quarters with many other families gave me a good opportunity to observe how people of different personalities behaved in stressful times. Some were optimists, who seemed to have the resilience to bounce back from their wartime losses with relative ease. They didn't dwell on their misfortunes, but moved on to lead productive lives, sharing their positive outlook with others. A perfect example was my math teacher, Jaan Raud, who maintained his positive outlook despite the tragedy that he and his wife experienced when their ship was sunk by a Soviet torpedo and they lost their unborn baby. His positive attitude was so contagious that it lifted the spirits of anyone who came to know him.

But there were a few others who commiserated and pined for what they had lost during the war. They were always unhappy and dissatisfied. This not only prevented them from leading fulfilling lives, but had a corrosive influence on others around them. After experiencing the vast difference between these two personalities, I have learned to appreciate the power a positive outlook can have on our lives.

Another factor that helped my family to survive the difficult journey was the generosity of people along the way. There were people who gave us food and shelter during our escape: the farmer in Hiiumaa, the veterinarian in Saaremaa, and Mrs. Oldekop in Jena. There were German volunteers in Danzig and Berlin, and generous families in America, who sent us clothing and CARE packages when we needed them. I will always be grateful to them. They helped us endure hardships and restored our faith in humanity during times when inhuman acts were routinely committed.

I was lucky to have the opportunity to come to the United States, where luck continued to be my frequent companion. I was fortunate to meet many talented and kind people who motivated me and generously shared their knowledge and wisdom. My lucky star was the brightest in Toronto when I met Siret, who has enriched my life in countless ways and helped me to see the world from a broader perspective than would have ever been possible alone.

I believe everyone in the United States is lucky to live in a free country. People who have always lived in a free world tend to take that freedom for granted. They may not appreciate it because they have never experienced the fear of someone knocking on their door in the middle of the night to take them away for no other reason than that they expressed their opinion or read the wrong book. Having survived two dictatorships, I know how precious freedom is. It is a gift worth nurturing and protecting with care.

Time Line

September 3: U.K. and France declare war on Germany

September 28: Soviet military bases established in Estonia

November 30: The Winter War between the Soviet Union and Finland begins

1940   *March 13:* The Winter War ends

June 16: Soviet ultimatum for entry of Soviet troops

June 17: 90,000 Soviet troops cross Estonian border

June 21: Pro-Soviet government formed

July 14–15: Fraudulent parliament elections

July 21: New parliament votes to join the Soviet Union

August 6: Annexation by the Soviet Union completed

1941   *June 14:* More than 10,000 Estonians deported to Siberia

June 22: Germany invades the Soviet Union

July 6: German Army reaches Estonian border

August 28: German Army enters Tallinn

September 15: New government formed under German military command

December 5: Estonia becomes part of German-occupied territory called Ostland

1943   *February 2:* German Army surrenders at Stalingrad

1944   *January 27:* The siege of Leningrad ends

March 9: Soviet air attack on Tallinn

June 6: Normandy invasion, D-Day

July 26: Soviet Army captures Narva

August 25: Soviet Army seizes Tartu

September 22: Soviet tanks enter Tallinn

September 24: Estonian mainland falls under Soviet control

1945   *May 8:* Germany surrenders to Allied Forces, V-E Day

1991   *August 20:* Estonia regains its independence

2004   *March 29:* Estonia becomes member of NATO

          May 1: Estonia joins the European Union

2011   *January 1:* Estonia joins eurozone

Acknowledgements

I would like to express my heartfelt gratitude to the people who helped me to make this book possible. First and foremost, my thanks go to Berteil Mahoney, who urged and encouraged me to write my story. Her memoir-writing workshop was an ideal environment for developing the first draft of the manuscript. Her steady support and constructive critiques, as well as the positive feedback of my fellow writers, were immeasurably valuable. I am truly grateful to all of them.

There were also some people from my past who helped me fill in a few gaps in my memory. Particularly helpful was Maie Kiive (nee Teene), the girl who travelled with us during our escape in September of 1944. With the aid of her diary, she was able to refresh my memory and correct some of my recollections of that journey. I am deeply grateful to her.

I would also like thank my classmate Malle Tael (nee Soolepp) of Oldenburg Estonian Gymnasium. My reminiscences with her about what happened in the displaced persons' camps evoked many memories that enriched the chapters describing those years. She also deserves credit for the photo of Camp Sandplatz.

Special thanks are due to my editors, Kimberly Bowcutt, for her excellent suggestions, and to Karen Palmer for saving me much embarrassment with her superb copyediting. I am also thankful to Denise Wada for her artistic design of the cover and maps.

I am profoundly grateful to my sister-in-law Maire Jaanus for her advice and thoughtful comments. My deepest thanks go to my wife Siret for her wisdom, loving support, and endless patience through the long process.

Made in the USA
San Bernardino, CA
18 December 2016